CITY COLLEGE LIBR
1825 MAY ST.
BROWNSVILLE, TEXAS 78520

T5-CAE-188

The
Garland Library
of
Narratives of
North American
Indian Captivities

Volume 95

311 titles in 111 volumes
selected and arranged by

Wilcomb E. Washburn

Director of the Office of American Studies
Smithsonian Institution

Contents

Two Months in the Camp of Big Bear

The life and adventures of Theresa Gowanlock and Theresa Delaney

Theresa Gowanlock

Garland Publishing Inc., New York & London

1976 CITY COLLEGE LIBRARY
1825 MAY ST.
BROWNSVILLE, TEXAS 78520

Copyright © 1976
by Garland Publishing, Inc.
All Rights Reserved

Bibliographical note:

this facsimile has been made from a copy in the
Newberry Library
(Ayer.256.G65.1885)

Library of Congress Cataloging in Publication Data

Gowanlock, Theresa.
    Two months in the camp of Big Bear.

    (The Garland library of narratives of North American
Indian captivities ; v. 95)
    Pt. 2 by T. Delaney.
    Reprint of the 1885 ed. published by the Times Office,
Parkdale.
    Issued with the reprint of the 1886 ed. of De Shields,
James T. Cynthia Ann Parker. New York, 1976.
    1. Cree Indians--Captivities. 2. Indians of North
America--Captivities. 3. Gowanlock, Theresa.
4. Delaney, Theresa Fulford. I. Delaney, Theresa
Fulford. II. Title.
E85.G2 vol. 95 [E99.C88] 973'.04'97s [970'.004'97] [B]
ISBN 0-8240-1719-6   75-40244

E
85
.G2
v.95

Printed in the United States of America

DEDICATED

TO

OUR SISTERS

THE

LADIES OF CANADA.

THE SCENE OF THE FROG LAKE MASSACRE.

Two Months in the

Camp of Big Bear.

The Life and Adventures

OF

Theresa Gowanlock and Theresa Delaney.

PART I.

PARKDALE:

TIMES OFFICE, 24 QUEEN STREET,

1885.

INTRODUCTION.

IT is not the desire of the author of this work to publish the incidents which drenched a peaceful and prosperous settlement in blood, and subjected the survivors to untold suffering and privations at the hands of savages, in order to gratify a morbid craving for notoriety. During all my perils and wanderings amid the snow and ice of that trackless prairie, the hope that nerved me to struggle on, was, that if rescued, I might within the sacred precincts of the paternal hearth, seek seclusion, where loving hands would help me to bear the burden of my sorrow, and try to make me forget at times, if they could not completely efface from my memory, the frightful scenes enacted around that prairie hamlet, which bereft me of my loved one, leaving my heart and fireside desolate for ever. Prostrated by fatigue and exposure, distracted by the constant dread of outrage and death, I had well-nigh abandoned all hope of ever escaping from the Indians with my life, but, as the darkness of the night is just before the dawn, so my fears which had increased until I was in despair, God in his inscrutible way speedily calmed, for while I was brooding over and preparing for my impending fate, a sudden commotion attracted my attention and in less time than it takes to write it, I was free. From that moment I received every kindness and attention, and as I approached the confines of civilization, I became aware of how diligently I had been sought after, and that for weeks I had been the object of the tenderest solicitude, not only of my friends and relations, but of the whole continent.

There have appeared so many conflicting statements in the public press regarding my capture and treatment while with the Indians, that it is my bounden duty to give to the public a truthful and accurate description of my capture, detention and misfortunes while captive in the camp of Big Bear. The task may be an irksome one and I might with justice shrink from anything which would recall the past. Still it is a debt of gratitude I owe to the people of this broad dominion. To the brave men who sacrificed their business and comfort and endured the hardships incident to a soldier's life, in order to vindicate the law. And to the noble men and women who planned for the comfort and supplied the wants of the gallant band who had so nobly responded to the call of duty and cry for help. And I gladly embrace this opportunity of showing to the public and especially the ladies, my appreciation of their kindness and sympathy in my bereavement, and their noble and disinterested efforts for my release. In undertaking a task which has no pleasures for me, and has been accomplished under the most trying difficulties and with the greatest physical suffering, I have embodied in the narrative a few of the manners and customs of Indians, the leading features of the country, only sufficient to render it clear and intelligible. I make no apology for issuing this volume to the public as their unabated interest make it manifest that they desire it, and I am only repaying a debt of gratitude by giving a truthful narrative to correct false impressions, for their kindness and sympathy to me.

I trust the public will receive the work in the spirit in which it is given and any literary defects which it may have, and I am sure there are many, may be overlooked, as I am only endeavoring to rectify error, instead of aspiring to literary excellence. I express my sincere and heartfelt thanks to the half-breeds who befriended me during my captivity, and to the friends and public generally who sheltered and assisted me in many ways and by many acts of kindness and sympathy, and whose attention was unremitting until I had reached my destination.

And now I must bid the public a grateful farewell and seek my wished for seclusion from which I would never have emerged but to perform a public duty.

THERESA GOWANLOCK.

MRS. GOWANLOCK.

Two Months in the Camp of Big Bear.

MRS. GOWANLOCK

CHAPTER I.

WE LEAVE ONTARIO.

W E left my father's house at Tintern on the 7th of October, 1884, having been married on the 1st, for Parkdale, where we spent a few days with my husband's friends. We started for our home on the 10th by the Canadian Pacific Railway to Owen Sound, thence by boat to Port Arthur, and then on to Winnipeg by rail, where we stopped one night going on the next day to Regina. We only stopped in that place one day, taking rail again to Swift Current, arriving there the same day. This ended our travel by the locomotion of steam.

After taking in a supply of provisions we made a start for Battleford, distant 195 miles, by buckboard over the prairie, which stretches out about 130 miles in length, and for the remaining 55 miles there are clumps of trees or bluffs as they are called, scattered here and there. Our journey over this part was very pleasant, the weather was fine and the mode of travelling, which was new to me, delightful. Our company, consisted in addition to ourselves, of only one person, Mr. Levalley, a gentleman from Ottawa. We passed four nights under canvas. The journey was not a lonely one, the ships of the prairie were continually on the go, we passed several companies of freighters with harnessed oxen, half-breeds and Indians. It was also full of incident and adventure ; on one occasion, when cooking our tea, we set fire to the prairie, although we worked hard to put it out, it in a very few minutes spread in a most alarming manner, and entirely beyond our control, and we let it go looking on enjoying the scene. Upon nearing Battleford a number of half-famished squaws came to us begging for something to eat, but we were not in a position, unfortunately, to supply their wants, on account of our larder having run dry. We entered Battleford on the 19th of October.

The town of Battleford is situated on the Battle river. The old on one side, the new on the other, in the direction of the fort. When the Indians plundered that place it was the town on the south bank. The houses on the opposite bank were protected by the guns at the fort. My husband had a store on the north bank in the direction of the fort.

The town is very scattered, covering a large area of ground, it is verily a place of distances and quite in keeping with the north-west generally. There are a few fine houses in the place, notably, the industrial home for Indian children and the residence of Judge Rolleau.

CHAPTER II.

INCIDENTS AT BATTLEFORD

I REMAINED at Battleford six weeks, while my husband went to Frog Creek, (where he had thirteen men working on the house and mills,) and while there I became initiated into the manners and customs of the inhabitants. A few incidents which happened during my stay might be interesting to the reader, therefore, I will jot them down as they come to mind.

After our arrival the Indians and squaws came to see me and would go and tell some of the others to come and see the monias, (squaw) and when they saw my husband they asked him why he did not live with her, and if she was well; and one day I walked with him over to where he was keeping store before he went west and the Indians came in and shook hands, and laughed, and the squaws thought my costume was rather odd and not in keeping with that of the fashionable north-western belle. The squaws cut off about three yards of print and make the skirt; while others take flour sacks and cut holes through for the waist and have leggings and moccasins; they would disdain to wear such an article as hose.

They are quite adepts in the art of tanning. I saw them tanning leather; they took the skin and put something on it, I do not know what it was, and put it in the sun for a few days, then with a small sharp iron fastened on a long handle, they scraped the skin with this until very smooth, and greased it over and put it in the sun again for some time, afterwards two squaws pulled it until nice and soft, and then it was ready for use.

One afternoon I was out shopping and on my way home

I saw some little Indian children coasting down hill on an earthen plate, but before getting to the end of the hill, to their evident surprise the plate broke and they commenced crying because it was broken and went back and got another one, and so on until they thought they would try tin plates, and the little friend that was with me, Effie Laurie, took the tin plate from them and sat down on it herself and went down the hill, and they looked so astonished to think that a white woman would do such a thing.

Another time on going out while two men were crossing the bridge over Battle river; a horse broke through and was killed and the squaws gathered around it taking the skin off, while others carried some of the carcass away, and I asked what they were going to do with it, and my husband said "they will take it home and have a big feast and if the meat has been poisoned they will boil it for a long time, changing the water, and in this way anything that was poisonous would not affect them."

The way the Indians get their wood, they send their squaws to the bush to cut the wood and they take a rope and tie around as much as they can carry, and hang it on their backs. Those who have dogs to carry the wood for them tie two long sticks together, fastening them on the dog's back, then tying a large bundle of wood on the back part of the cross sticks by that means the squaw is relieved from the task. The squaws perform all manual labor, while the big, lazy, good-for-nothing Indian lolls about in idleness.

BEASTS OF BURDEN.

CHAPTER III.

ON TO OUR HOME.

AT the end of six weeks my husband returned from the west, and with many pleasant recollections of Battleford, we left for our own home, which I had pictured in my mind with joyous anticipation, as the place of our continued happiness; a beautiful oasis, in that land of prairie and sparse settlement, and with a buoyancy of spirit which true happiness alone can bring, I looked forward with anticipated pleasure, which made that little log house appear to me, a palace, and we its king and queen.

On this last part of our journey we were favored with the company of Mr. Ballentyne of Battleford who went with us, and after the first day's travelling, we stopped all night at a half-breed's house, where they had a large fire-place made of mud, which was just like a solid piece of stone; they had a bright fire, and everything appeared nice and tidy within; a woman was making bannock, and when she had the dough prepared, she took a frying pan and put the cake in and stood it up before the fire. This is the way they do all their baking, and then she fried some nice white fish and hung a little kettle on a long iron hook over the fire, put in potatoes, and boiled the tea-kettle, making the tea in it too. She then spread a white cloth over the table and we all enjoyed our supper together after the long ride. The squaw gave us a nice clean bed to sleep in, making theirs on the floor and in the morning I saw four little children crawling out from under the bed where we slept, and my husband looked up at me and laughed, and said, "that is where children sleep up in *this country.*" Their ways appeared very strange to me, and in the morning before going away, they gave us a warm breakfast.

We travelled all the next day and camped that night. We had a small tin stove which is part of a camping outfit, and which smoked very much while cooking.   We had great trouble to know how we would obtain a light, but we had a candle and we lighted that, and then we had nothing to hold it in, but as necessity is the mother of invention, we found a way out of the difficulty ; we took a pocket knife that had two blades, and stuck one blade in the tent pole and opened the other half way, fastening the candle into the blade, which answered the purpose and enabled us to see while we ate our supper.   We then turned down our beds, and in a few minutes were fast asleep.   When morning came we had breakfast, and travelled on again.   Mr. Ballentyne shot some prairie chickens and we had them for our dinner, which was a great treat to me.   We arrived at Fort Pitt on the tenth, bidding Mr. Ballentyne good-bye, stopped at Mr. McLean's all night, where we enjoyed a very pleasant evening.

The next morning we left for Onion Lake, where we were welcomed by Mr. Mann and family, and after a night's rest proceeded on our journey to Frog Lake, reaching there on the 12th.   We went to Mr. and Mrs. Delaney's, who kindly allowed me to stop there until my husband fixed up some articles of furniture at our own house two miles further on and south-west of the Lake.

After arriving at Mrs. Delaney's, my husband left me and went down to the house to work ; on Saturday evening he came back.   On Sunday morning Mr. Quinn came over and asked us to go for a drive, we accepted the invitation. It was a bright frosty morning ; he took us to our little home that I had not yet seen.   On hearing the men singing who were employed at the mill, we drove down to their cooking tent, where we found Mr. Gilchrist cooking breakfast for fourteen men.   They had a large cooking stove inside, with a long board table; the table was covered with tin plates and cups. They had rabbit soup, and bread and coffee for breakfast; after getting ourselves warm we drove back to Mr. Delaney's. On the following Thursday my husband drove up and took me to our home, where all was in beautiful order, and Mr. Gilchrist waiting for our arrival.

CHAPTER IV.

AT HOME.

NOW we are at home and I am thankful. There they nestle in a pretty valley, the simple house, the store, and beside the brook, the mill. The music of the workman's hammer alone breaks the stillness that pervades the scene, and the hills send back the echo without a discordant note. The hills were covered with trees, principally poplar and spruce, interspersed with berry-bearing shrubs. A most beautiful and enchanting location.

That little settlement of our own was situated upon Frog Creek, about three miles west of the lake of the same name, and distant from the Frog Lake Settlement, our nearest white neighbours, about two miles. But we had neighbours close by, who came in to see us the next day, shaking hands and chatting to us in Cree, of which language we knew but little. The Indians appeared to be very kind and supplied us with white fish twice a week which they procured from the river for which in return we gave sugar, tea, prints, &c., from the store. Christmas and New Year's were celebrated in about the same manner that they are amongst us civilized people. Both Indians and squaws put on their good clothes, which at the best of times is very scant, and do their calling. They salute the inmates of each house they enter with a congratulatory shake, expecting to be kissed in return. Just think of having to kiss a whole tribe of Indians in one day, that part we would rather do by proxy. We would not countenance it in any way.

On Christmas day we went out for a walk along Frog Creek ; on our way we came to where two little Indian children were catching rabbits with a snare, they stepped to

CITY COLLEGE LIBRARY
1825 MAY ST.
BROWNSVILLE, TEXAS 78520

one side and let us pass, and were delighted to have us watching them while catching their game ; and further on some of the squaws had holes cut in the ice, and having a sharp hook were catching fish. In this way they get fish all winter, and to look at these "shrimpy-looking" women trotting along with their brown babies slung in a sort of loose pocket dangling away behind their backs, it was comical in the extreme, they would stop and look and laugh at us, our appearance being so very different to their own dark skin and sharp eyes. They wear their hair hanging, strung with brass beads, and have small pieces of rabbit fur tied in; and the men wear theirs cut very short in front, hanging over their brows, and ornaments of every description. These people don't set at table on chairs, rich or poor ; they squat down on their feet in a fashion that would soon tire us exceedingly. Then at night they wrap themselves up in a blanket, lie down and sleep as soundly as we would in our warm feather bed and blankets.

My husband and the men worked hard during the next two months on the mill in order to get it finished before the spring set in. As far as the weather was concerned it was very favourable for working. The men lost no time from the cold. During that period the thermometer ranged from zero to 60° below but the air was so clear and bracing that the cold was never felt. I have experienced more severe weather in Ontario than I ever did in this part. I have heard of north-west blizzards, but they are confined to the prairie and did not reach us. It is the most beautiful country I ever saw with its towering hills, majestic rivers, beautiful flowers and rolling land. I had made up my mind to see nothing but frost, ice and snow, but was agreeably disappointed.

Nothing of an eventful nature transpired, during those two months, the mill was about completed and Williscraft and the other men were discharged with the exception of Mr. Gilchrist, who assisted my husband.   The machinery was all in position and everything done but finishing up, when on the 17th of March, two men, strangers, made their appearance at the mill and asked for employment.   They said they were weary and worn and had left Duck Lake in order to avoid the trouble that was brewing there.   One was Gregory Donaire and the other Peter Blondin, my husband took pity on them and gave them employment.   They worked for us until the massacre.   They were continually going too and fro among the Indians, and I cannot but believe, that they were cognizant of everything that was going on, if not responsible in a great degree for the murders which were afterwards committed.

CHAPTER V.

WOOD AND PLAIN INDIANS.

THE Indians are in their habits very unclean and filthy. They will not in the least impress anyone to such an extent that they would be willing to forego the restrictions of civilized life, and enter upon the free life of the red man.

The Indians living on the reserve in the neighbourhood of Frog Creek are known as the Wood Crees, they were all peaceable and industrious, and were becoming proficient in the art of husbandry. They lived in the log cabins in the winter, but in the summer they took to their tents. They numbered about 200 persons. They appeared satisfied with their position which was much better than what falls to the lot of other Indians. They did not take part in the massacre, nor where they responsible for it in any way.

The Plain Crees are composed of the worst characters from all the tribes of that name. They were dissatisfied, revengeful, and cruel, they could not be persuaded to select their reserve until lately, and then they would not settle upon it. Their tastes lay in a direction the opposite to domestic ; they were idle and worthless, and were the Indians who killed our dear ones on that ever to be remembered 2nd of April. Those same Indians were constantly fed by Mr. Delaney and my husband. The following correspondence will show how he treated those ungrateful characters:—Big Bear's Indians were sent up to Frog Lake, it is said, by Governer Dewdney who told them, if they would go there, they would never be hungry, but last winter their rations were stopped, and they had to work to get provisions, or starve. They would go around to the settlers' houses and ask for something to eat, and Mr. Delaney would give those Indians rations, paying for them out of his own salary.   Gov. Dewdney wrote a letter stating that he must stop it at once ; but he did not listen to him and kept on giving to them until the outbreak.   And the very men he befriended were the ones who hurled him into sudden death.

Big Bear was only nominally the chief of this tribe, the ruling power being in the hands of Wandering Spirit, a bad and vicious man, who exercised it with all the craft and cunning of an accomplished freebooter.

CHAPTER VI.

THE MASSACRE.

NOW come the dreadful scenes of blood and cruel death. The happy life is changed to one of suffering and sorrow. The few months of happiness I enjoyed with the one I loved above all others was abruptly closed—taken from me for ever—it was cruel, it was dreadful. When I look back to it all, I often wonder, is it all a dream, and has it really taken place. Yes, the dream is too true; it is a terrible reality, and as such will never leave my heart, or be effaced from off my mind.

The first news we heard of the Duck Lake affair was on the 30th of March. Mr. Quinn, the Indian Agent, at Frog Lake, wrote a letter to us and sent it down to our house about twelve o'clock at night with John Pritchard, telling my husband and I to go up to Mr. Delaney's on Tuesday morning, and with his wife go on to Fort Pitt, and if they saw any excitement they would follow. We did not expect anything to occur. When we got up to Mr. Delaney's we found the police had left for Fort Pitt. Big Bear's Indians were in the house talking to Mr. Quinn about the trouble at Duck Lake, and saying that Poundmaker the chief at Battleford wanted Big Bear to join him but he would not, as he intended remaining where he was and live peaceably. They considered Big Bear to be a better man than he was given credit for.

On the 1st of April they were in, making April fools of the white people and shaking hands, and they thought I was frightened and told me not to be afraid, because they would not hurt us. My husband left me at Mr. Delaney's and went back to his work at the mill, returning in the evening with Mr. Gilchrist. We all sat talking for some

time along with Mr. Dill, who had a store at Frog Lake
and Mr. Cameron, clerk for the Hudson Bay Company.
We all felt perfectly safe where we were, saying that as we
were so far away from the trouble at Duck Lake, the Government would likely come to some terms with them and the
affair be settled at once.   The young Chief and another
Indian by the name of Isador said if anything was wrong
among Big Bear's band they would come and tell us; and
that night Big Bear's braves heard about it and watched
them all night to keep them from telling us.   We all went
to bed not feeling in any way alarmed.   About five o'clock
in the morning a rap came to the door and Mr. Delaney
went down stairs and opened it, and John Pritchard and
one of Big Bear's sons by the name of Ibesies were there.

Pritchard said " There trouble."

Mr. Delaney said " Where ? "

Pritchard "*Here !*   Our horses are all gone, the Indians
deceived us, and said that some half-breeds from Edmonton had come in the night and had taken them to Duck
Lake, but Big Bear's band has taken them and hid them,
I am afraid it is all up."

My husband and I got up, and Mrs. Delaney came down
stairs with a frightened look.   In a few minutes Big Bear's
Indians were all in the house, and had taken all the arms
from the men saying they were going to protect us from the
half-breeds, and then we felt we were being deceived.   They
took all the men over to Mr. Quinn's, and my husband and I
were sitting on the lounge, and an Indian came in and
took him by the arm saying he wanted him to go too; and
he said to Mrs. Delaney and I "do not to be afraid, while I
go with this Indian." We stopped in the house, and while
they were gone some of the Indians came in and went
through the cupboard to find something to eat. They opened
the trap door to go down cellar, but it was very dark, and

they were afraid to venture down. Then the men
came back and Mrs. Delaney got breakfast. We all
sat down, but I could not eat, and an Indian asked Mr.
Gowanlock to tell me not to be afraid, they would not hurt
us, and I should eat plenty. After breakfast they took us
out of the house and escorted us over to the church; my
husband taking my arm, Mr. and Mrs. Delaney were walking beside us. When we got to the church the priests were
holding mass; it was Holy Thursday, and as we entered the
door, Wandering Spirit sat on his knees with his gun; he was
painted, and had on such a wicked look. The priests did
not finish the service on account of the menacing manner
of the Indians; they were both around and inside the
church. We were all very much frightened by their behaviour. They then told us to go out of the church, and
took us back to Mr. Delaney's, all the Indians going in too.
We stopped there for awhile and an Indian came and told
us to come out again, and my husband came to me and
said "you had better put your shawl around you, for its very
cold, perhaps we will not be gone long." We all went out with
the Indians. They were going through all the stores.
Everything was given to them, and they got everything they
could wish for and took us up the hill towards their camp.
We had only gone but a short distance from the house when
we heard the reports of guns, but thought they were firing in
the air to frighten us; but they had shot Quinn, Dill and
Gilchrist, whom I did not see fall. Mr. and Mrs. Delaney
were a short distance ahead of my husband, I having my
husband's arm. Mr. Williscraft, an old grey-headed man
about seventy-five years of age came running by us, and
an Indian shot at him and knocked his hat off, and he turned
around and said, *"Oh ! don't shoot! don't shoot!"* But they
fired again, and he ran screaming and fell in some bushes.
On seeing this I began crying, and my husband tried to

comfort me, saying, "my *dear* wife be *brave* to the end," and immediately an Indian behind us fired, and my husband fell beside me his arm pulling from mine. I tried to assist him from falling. He put out his arms for me and fell, and I fell down beside him and buried my face on his, while his life was ebbing away so quickly, and was prepared for the next shot myself, thinking I was going with him too. But death just then was not ordained for me. I had yet to live. An Indian came and took me away from my dying husband side, and I refused to leave. Oh! to think of leaving my *dear* husband lying there for those cruel Indians to dance around. I begged of the Indian to let me stay with him, but he took my arm and pulled me away. Just before this, I saw Mr. Delaney and a priest fall, and Mrs. Delaney was taken away in the same manner that I was. I still looking back to where my poor husband was lying dead; the Indian motioned to where he was going to take me, and on we went. I thought my heart would break; I would rather have died with my husband and been at rest.

> " A rest that is sure for us all,
> But sweeter to some."

CHAPTER VII.

WITH THE INDIANS.

HARDLY knowing how I went or what I did, I trudged along in a half conscious condition. Led a captive into the camp of Big Bear by one of his vile band. Taken through brush and briar, a large pond came to view, we did not pass it by, he made me go through the water on that cold 2nd of April nearly to my waist. I got so very weak that I could not walk and the Indian pulled me along, in this way he managed to get me to his tepee. On seeing Mrs. Delaney taken away so far from me, I asked the Indian to take me to her; and he said "*No, No,*" and opening the tent shoved me in. A friendly squaw put down a rabbit robe for me to sit on ; I was shivering with the cold ; this squaw took my shoes and stockings off and partly dried them for me. Their tepees consisted of long poles covered with smoke-stained canvas with two openings, one at the top for a smoke hole and the other at the bottom for a door through which I had to crawl in order to enter. In the centre they have their fire; this squaw took a long stick and took out a large piece of beef from the kettle and offered it to me, which I refused, as I could not eat anything after what I had gone through.

Just then Big Bear's braves came into the tent; there were nearly thirty of them, covered with war paint, some having on my husband's clothes, and all giving vent to those terrible yelis, and holding most murderous looking instruments. They were long wooden clubs. At one end were set three sharp shining knife blades. They all looked at me as I eyed those weapons (and they well matched the expression of their cruel mouths and develish eyes) thinking my troubles would soon be over I calmly awaited the result.

But they sat down around me with a bottle full of something that looked like water, passing it from one Indian to the other, so I put on a brave look as if I was not afraid of them. After this they all went out and the most blood-curdling yells that ever pierced my ears was their war-whoop, mingled with dancing and yelling and cutting most foolish antics.

I saw a little baby that I thought must be dead, lying in one part of the tent, they had it done up in a moss bag. I will try and give an idea of what it was like: they take a piece of cloth having it large at the top, and cut it around where the feet should be, and on both sides of this little bag they have loops of very fine leather, then they have a small thin cushion laid on this the length of the child, and three or four pieces of different colored flannels, then they dress the baby in a thin print gown and put it in this bag, and its little legs are put down just as straight as a needle, covered over with moss, which they first heat very hot ; then the arms are put down in the same way and the flannels are wrapped around very tight and then they lace the bag up, and all that can be seen is the little brown face peeping out.

Just then Pritchard's little girl came in where I was ; she could talk a few words of English. I asked her where her pa was, and she said that he was putting up a tent not far away, and then I had some hope of getting from the Indians.

After I had been there for four hours, Louis Goulet and Andre Nault came in, and Goulet said to me "Mrs. Gowanlock if you will give yourself over to the half-breeds, they will not hurt you; Peter Blondin has gone down to where the mill is, and when he comes back he will give his horse for you." I asked them to interpret it to the Indians in order to let me go to Pritchard's tent for awhile, and the Indians said that she could go with this squaw. I went and was overjoyed to see Mrs. Delaney there also. After getting in there

I was unconscious for a long time, and upon coming to my senses, I found Mrs. Pritchard bathing my face with cold water. When Blondin came back he gave his horse and thirty dollars for Mrs. Delaney and me. He put up a tent and asked me to go with him, but I refused ; and he became angry and did everything he could to injure me. That man treated me most shamefully; if it had not been for Pritchard I do not know what would have become of me. Pritchard was kinder than any of the others.

After I had been a prisoner three days, Blondin came and asked me if I could ride horse back, and I said "yes," and he said if I would go with him, he would go and take two of the best horses that Big Bear had and desert that night. I told him I would *never* leave Pritchard's tent until we all left, saying "I would go and drown myself in the river before I would go with him."

Late that same night a French Canadian by the name of Pierre came into the tent, and hid himself behind us, he said the Indians wanted to shoot him, and some one told him to go and hide himself, ultimately one of the half-breeds gave a horse to save his life. Mrs. Pritchard told him not to stay in there. She did not want to see any more men killed, and one of the half-breeds took him away and he was placed under the protection of the Wood Crees. This man had been working with Goulet and Nault all winter getting out logs about thirty miles from Frog Lake.

CHAPTER VIII.

PROTECTED BY HALF-BREEDS.

ON the 3rd of April Big Bear came into our tent and sitting down beside us told us he was very sorry for what had happened, and cried over it, saying he knew he had so many bad men but had no control over them.   He came very often to our tent telling us to "eat and sleep plenty, they would not treat us like the white man.   The white man when he make prisoner of Indian, he starve him and cut his hair off."   He told us he would protect us if the police came.   The same day Big Bear's braves paid our tent another visit, they came in and around us with their guns, knives and tomahawks, looking at us so wickedly.

Pritchard said, "For God sake let these poor women live, they can do no harm to you ; let them go home to their friends."

The leaders held a brief consultation.

An Indian stood up and pointing to the heavens said, "We promise by God that we will not hurt these white women ; we will let them live."

They then left the tent.

Every time I saw one of Big Bear's Indians coming in, I expected it was to kill us, or take us away from the tent, which would have been *far worse* than death to *me*.

But they did not keep their word.

On the third night (Saturday, the 4th April,) after our captivity, two Indians came in while all the men and Mrs. Delaney were asleep, I heard them, and thought it was Pritchard fixing the harness, he usually sat up to protect us.

A match was lighted and I saw two of the most hedious look-ing Indians looking over and saying where is the *Monias.* squaw, meaning the white women.   I got so frightened I could not move, but Mrs. Delaney put out her foot and awak-ened Mrs. Pritchard, and she wakened her husband, and he started up and asked what they wanted, and they said they wanted to take the white women to their tent, and I told Pritchard they could kill me before I would go, and I prayed to God to help me.   Pritchard and Adolphus Nolin gave their blankets and dishes and Mrs. Pritchard, took the best blanket off her bed to give to them and they went off, and in the morning the Wood Crees came in and asked if those Indians took much from us, and Pritchard told them "No" ; the Indians wanted to make them give them back.   After that Pritchard and other half-breeds protected us from night to night for we were not safe a single minute.

During the two days which had passed, the bodies of the men that were murdered had not been buried.   They were lying on the road exposed to the view of everyone.   The half-breeds carried them off the road to the side, but the Indians coming along dragged them out again.   It was dreadful to see the bodies of our *poor dear* husbands dragged back and forth by those demoniac savages.

On Saturday the day before Easter, we induced some half-breeds to take our husbands' bodies and bury them.   They placed them, with those of the priests, under the church. The Indians would not allow the other bodies to be moved. And dreadful to relate those inhuman wretches set fire to. the church, and with yelling and dancing witnessed it burn to the ground.   The bodies, I afterwards heard, were charred beyond recognition.

Upon seeing what was done the tears ran profusely down our cheeks and I thought my very heart would break.   All the comfort we received from that unfeeling band was, "that's right, cry plenty, we have killed your husbands and we will soon have you."

On Easter Sunday night there was a heavy thunder storm and before morning it turned cold and snowed ; the tent pole broke, coming down within an inch of my head, the snow blowing in and our bedding all covered with it and nothing to keep us warm. I got up in the morning and found my shoes all wet and frozen, and the Indians came in and told us what they saw in the heavens. They saw a church and a man on a large black horse with his arm out and he looked so angry, and they said God must be angry with them for doing such a thing ; the half-breeds are as superstitious as the Indians.

CHAPTER IX.

THEY TAKE FORT PITT.

THE morning of the 6th of April was a memorable one. Something unusual was going to take place from the excited state of the camp. Everyone was on the go. I was in a short time made acquainted with the reason. It was more blood, more butchery, and more treachery. And oh! such a sight presented itself to my eyes. The Indians were all attired in full war habiliments. They had removed their clothes. A girdle around their waists, was all—and their paint—every shade and color. Heads with feathers, and those who had killed a white, with quills. A quill for every man scalped. Eyes painted like stars, in red, yellow and green; faces, arms, legs and bodies elaborately decorated, and frescoed in all their savage beauty, with bars, spots, rings and dots. Brandishing tomahawks, bludgeons and guns; flinging and firing them in every direction, accompanied with yells and whoops; a most hideous and terrible sight. They embraced their wives and children, and the command was given to start for Fort Pitt. In order to swell their numbers they compelled the half-breeds and some of their squaws to accompany them. The squaws ride horses like the men.

On Sunday the 12th of April they returned from the Fort flush with victory. They had captured that place, killed policeman Cowan, taken the whites prisoners, and allowed the police to escape down the river, all without loosing an Indian or half-breed. The prisoners were brought in while we were at dinner. Mr. and Mrs. Quinney came to our tent. Mrs. Quinney said she was cold and wet. She sat down and put her arms around me and cried. I gave her a cup of hot tea and something to eat. Shortly after the Mc-

Lean's and Mann's came in. It was a great relief to see white people again.

It was not long before they moved camp about two miles from Frog Lake. Mrs. Delaney and I, walking with Mrs. Pritchard and family, through mud and water; my shoes were very thin, and my feet very wet and sore from walking. The Indians were riding beside us with our horses and buckboards, laughing and jeering at us with umbrellas over their heads and buffalo overcoats on. We would laugh and make them believe we were enjoying it, and my heart ready to break with grief all the time. When we camped, it was in a circle. A space in the centre being kept for dancing.

I asked Blondin if he had any of our stockings or underclothing in his sacks. He told me *no*, and shortly afterwards took out a pair of my husband's long stockings and put them on before me, he would change them three and four times a week. He had nearly all my poor husband's clothes. Two men came in one time while Blondin was asleep and took one of my husband's coats out of his sack and went out; Blondin upon missing it got very angry and swore before me, saying that some person had come in and taken one of his coats, and all the time I knew whose coat it was they were quarrelling over. I wished then I could close my eyes and go home to God. I went outside the tent and saw this other half-breed named Gregory Donaire with my husband's coat on and pants, and just as I looked up I thought it must be my own husband, and to see the fellow laugh in my face, he evidently had an idea about what I was thinking. Blondin wore my husband's overcoat, and all I had was my little shawl and nothing to wear on my head, and the rain pouring down in torrents on me; this fellow would walk beside the waggon and laugh, and when it quit raining asked

3

me if I wanted *his* overcoat; I told him *no*, I did not mind being wet as much as he did. That night Mrs. Delaney and I lay down in one corner of the tent until morning came and then we had all the baking to do. We dug a hole in the ground and started a fire, taking flour, we stirred in water, kneading it hard. We then with our hands flattened it out and placed it in a frying pan, baking it before the fire, and by the time it was baked it was as black as the pan itself. We dined on bannock and bacon for two months, and were very thankful to get it.

CHAPTER X.

COOKING FOR A LARGE FAMILY.

MY experience of camp life was of such a character, that I would rather be a maid-of-all-work in any position than slush in an Indian tepee, reeking as it is, with filth and poisonous odors. There is no such a thing as an health officer among that band of braves. They have a half spirit-ualized personage whom they designate the Medicine Man; but he is nothing more or less than a quack of the worst kind. As in every other part of their life, so in the domestic they were unclean.

One evening, just as we had everything ready for our meal, in rushed the Big Bear's, gobbling up every-thing. After they had gone, I set to work to wash the dish-es. . Mrs. Pritchard thereat became quite angry, and would not allow me, saying that we would be glad to do more than that for the Indians yet. I went without my supper that night; I would rather starve than eat after that dirty horde.

One day, Pritchard brought in a rabbit for dinner. I thought we were going to have a treat as well as a good meal; we were engaged at other work that day, and Mrs. Pritchard did the cooking herself, but I had occasion to go in the direc-tion of the fire, and there was the rabbit in the pot boiling, it was all there, head, eyes, feet, and everything together. My good dinner vanished there and then. I told Mrs. Delaney there was no rabbit for me. I only ate to keep myself alive and well, for if I showed signs of sickness I would have been put with the Indians, and they would have put an end to me in a short time.

We had fifteen in our tent to bake for, besides the Indians, that came in to gorge, about thirty at a time. We cut wood and carried water and did Mrs. Pritchard sewing for her nine children; making their clothing that came from our own house. She took some muslin that Mrs. Delaney had bought before the trouble, and cut it up into aprons for her little baby, and gave me to make, and then she went to the trunk that had all my lace trimming that I had made through the winter, and brought some for me to sew on the aprons. I made them up as neatly as I possibly could, and when finished, she thanked me for it. The little children played with keepsakes that my *mother* had given to me when a little girl, and I had to look and see them broken in pieces without a murmur, also see my friends photographs thrown around and destroyed. I gathered up a few that were scattered around in the dirt and saved them when no one was looking

If Big Bear's braves would say move camp immediately, and if we should be eating and our tent not taken down just then, they would shout in the air and come and tear it down. In travelling, the Indians ride, and their squaws walk and do all the work, and they pack their dogs and have "travores" on their horses, upon which they tied their little children, and then all would move off together; dogs howling, and babies crying, and Indians beating their wives, and carts tumbling over the banks of the trail, and children falling, and horses and oxen getting mired down in the mud, and squaws cutting sacks of flour open to get a piece of cotton for string, and leaving the flour and throwing away the provisions, while others would come along and gather it up. We rode on a lumber waggon, with an ox team, and some of the squaws thought we did not work enough. Not work enough, after walking or working all day, after dark we were required to bake bannock and do anything else they had a mind to give us. They wanted to work us to death.

CHAPTER XI.

INCIDENTS BY THE WAY.

THE Indians are not only vicious, treacherous and super-stitious, but they are childlike and simple, as the following incident will show:—After the Indians came back from Fort Pitt, one of them found a glass eye; that eye was the favorite optic of Stanley Simpson, who was taken a prisoner there by Big Bear. He brought it with him for one of his brother Indians who was blind in one eye, imagining with untutored wisdom that if it gave light to a white man, it should also to a red, and they worked at it for a time, but they could not get the focus, finally they threw it away, saying it was no good, he could not see.

While we were in camp, Mr. Quinn's little two year old girl would come in and put her little arms around our necks and kiss us. The dear little thing had no one to care for her, she would stay with us until her mother would come and take her away. The squaws also carried her around on their backs with nothing but a thin print dress on and in her bare feet. How I did feel for her, she was such a bright little girl, her father when alive took care of her. It was very hard to see her going around like any of the Indian children.

One day while travelling we came to a large creek and had to get off the waggon and pull our shoes and stockings off in order that they would be dry to put on after we got across; the water was up to our waists and we waded through. Miss McLean took her little three year old sister on her back and carried her over. After crossing we had to walk a long distance on the burnt prairie to get to the waggon, then we sat down and put our shoes on. Some of the Indians coming along said, "oh! see the monais squaw." We would laugh, tell them it was nice ; that we enjoyed it. If they thought we did not, we were in danger of being taken away by them and made to work for them like their squaws.

One of Big Bear's son's wives died, and they dug a hole in the ground and wrapped blankets around her, and laid her in it, and put sacks of bacon and flour on top so that she could not get out, they covered her over with earth; and watched the place for some time for fear she would come to life again.

Their dances occur every day, they go and pick out the largest tents and go and take them from the Wood Crees, and leave them all day without any covering, with the white people who were prisoners, with them. They thought the white people took it as an honor to them, and every time in moving, Big Bear's band would tell us just where to put our tents, and if one camped outside this circle, they would go and cut their tent in pieces. In some of their dances Little Poplar was arrayed in some of Miss McLean's ribbons, ties and shawls, another with my hat on, and another with Mrs. Delaney's, and the squaws with our dresses, and they had a large dish of meat in the centre and danced awhile, and sat down and ate and danced again, keeping this up all day long. And if anyone lagged in the dance, it was a bad day for him. Little Poplar had a whip, and he would ply it thick on the back of the sluggish dancer.

One day just as we were eating dinner, an Indian came and invited us out to a dog feast; the men went, but we preferred bannock and bacon, to dog. They sent each of us *three yards* of print to make us a dress ; a squaw takes no more than that. And then a friendly Indian made me a present of a pair of green glasses.

A most dreadful affair occurred one day, they killed one of their squaws, an old grey headed woman that was insane.

The Indians and half-breeds were afraid of her, and she told them if they did not kill her before the sun went down, she would eat the whole camp up. They got some of the half-breeds to tie her, and they carried her out on a hill, and one old half-breed struck her on the head, and the Indians shot her in the head three times, cut it off and set fire to it; they were very much afraid she would come back and do some harm to them.

One evening after making our bed for the night, four squaws came into our tent and sat down for two hours, crying and singing and clapping their hands, and after going out, some of the Indians took and tied them until morning; it was a most strange procedure. I could go on enumerating incident after incident, but I have, I think, given sufficient to give the reader an insight into their character.

CHAPTER XII.

DANCING PARTIES.

WHILE we were on the way too Fort Pitt, a letter was received from the Rev. John McDougall, of Calgary, stating that troops were coming through from Edmonton, and that they would make short work of Big Bear's band for the murders they had committed at Frog Lake. They were terribly frightened at that news, and took turns and watched on the hills night and day. Others spent their time in dancing—it was dancing all the time—all day and all night.

I will explain their mode of dancing as well as I can:— They all get in a circle, while two sit down outside and play the tom-tom, a most unmelodious instrument, something like a tambourine, only not half so *sweet*; it is made in this way:—they take a hoop or the lid of a butter firkin, and cover one side with a very thin skin, while the other has strings fastened across from side to side, and upon this they pound with sticks with all their might, making a most unearthly racket. The whole being a fit emblem of what is going on in the other world of unclean spirits. Those forming the circle, kept going around shouting and kicking, with all the actions and paraphernalia of a clown in a pantomine, only not so dumb.

We passed a short distance from where Mrs. Delaney lived, and all we could see standing, was the bell of the Catholic Mission, and when we came to Onion Lake, they had burnt some of the buildings there, and as we passed they set fire to the rest. They burnt all the flour and potatoes, some three hundred sacks, and when we reached Fort Pitt our provisions were getting scarce, and the half-breeds went to the Fort to get some flour, but the Indians had previously poured coal

and machine oil on what was left, and they only got a few
sacks and not very clean at that. Still we felt very thankful
to have it as it was.

While in this neighbourhood, Blondin and Henry Quinn
went down to the river to make their escape, and Blondin
well knew that the Indians had said if one prisoner ran away
they would kill all the rest. The half-breeds hearing what
they had done, went after them and brought them back, and
that night Big Bear's braves came into our tent where Quinn
and Blondin were, and wanted to go to work and cut Quinn
in pieces. Blondin was like one of themselves. Pritchard
sat on his knees in front of Quinn and kept them from doing
it. They were in our tent nearly the whole night with their
guns, large sharp knives and war clubs. After Pritchard had
talked some hours to them they went out only partly pacified.
Some of them said, " he has ran away once, let us kill him
and have no more trouble with him ; if he runs away he will
be going away and telling the police to come."

When near the Fort they had their " Thirst Dance." An
Indian went to the bush and broke off a green bough, and
carried it to the place arranged for the dance, and all the
other Indians shot at it. Then the Indians got their
squaws with them on horse-back ; some thought it would
not be polite if they did not invite the white women to
help them also, and Mrs. Pritchard and another squaw came in
and put Mrs. Delaney in one corner and covered her over,
and me in another with a feather bed over me, so as not to find
us. Then some said " Oh, let the white women stay where
they are," and they took their squaws and went to the woods.
I should say about fifty rode to the woods for one stick at a
time, fastening a chain around it, dragged it along to this
place singing and yelling as they went. After they had
enough sticks, they arranged a tent in the centre of the circle.
They stood a long pole up, and on this pole they tied every-

thing they wished to give to the *sun*, and this is never taken down, and then they erected smaller poles about five feet high, all around in a large circle, and from the top of these they fastened sticks to the long pole in the centre, and covered it all with green boughs, they then partitioned the tent into small stalls, and tied print and anything bright all around inside on these poles; after they had this arranged they began dancing. It continues three days and three nights, neither eating or drinking during the entertainment. They danced all that night and the squaws had each a small whistle made of bone which they blow all the time in addition to the musical "tom-toms." Mrs. Delaney and I lay awake all night, and I said to her, "I hope the police will come in while they are having this dance." Mrs. Pritchard asked us next morning if we would go and see them at it, and remarked " they will not like it if you white women do not go and see them." We went with her, and when we got inside they laughed and were delighted at seeing us come. There they were, some of the squaws with my clothes on, and one Indian with my husband's on, and my table linen hanging on the poles. The squaws stood in those little stalls and danced. They had their faces painted, and fingers and ears filled with brass rings and thimbles. Some of the Indians were dressed in the police uniforms and had veils over their faces; and just as we got nicely there, two Indians came riding around and saying the police were all on this side of the river with their tents pitched. There must be hundreds of them, some said, and the others said *no*, because they have their wives and children with them; and then came the scattering, they ran in all directions like scared rabbits and tore their tents down, the Indians riding around on horse-back singing and yelling, and saying "let us go and meet them" that was to fight, and others said "*no*, let us move," and we all left and moved through the woods.

But it proved to be more than a mere scare.   *Our* friends were drawing near—too near to to be comfortable for the *noble* "red man," the murderers of defenceless settlers, the despoilers of happy homes, the polluters of poor women and children.   They did all that, and yet they are called the noble "red man."   It might sound musical in the ears of the poet to write of the virtues of that race, but I consider it a perversion of the real facts.   During the time I was with them I could not see anything noble in them, unless it was that they were *noble* murderers, *noble* cowards, *noble* thieves. The facts, I think, also go to show that the Indians are not treated properly.   There is no distinction made between the good (there are good Indians) and bad.   The character of the Indian is not studied sufficiently, or only so far as self-interest and selfish motives are concerned.   But the majority of the present race can be designated anything but the noble "red man."

They would in many instances, be better without the missionary.   If all denominations would only amalgamate their forces and agree upon an unsectarian basis for missionary effort, the Indians would become evangalized more quickly then they are at present.   It would be better for the Indians, and more honorable for the Christian Church.   Give the Indians the Gospel in its simplicity without the ritual of the denominations.

CHAPTER XIII

ANOTHER BATTLE.

WAS it the distant roar of heaven's artillery that caught my ear. I listened and heard it again. The Indians heard it and were frightened.

A half-breed in a stage whisper cried, "a cannon! a cannon!"

An Indian answered, "a cannon is no good to fight."

I looked at them and it showed them to be a startled and fear-stricken company, notwithstanding that they held the cannon with such disdain as to say "cannon no good to fight." That night was full of excitement for the Indians; they felt that the enemy was drawing near, too close in fact to be safe. The prisoners were excited with the thought, that perhaps there was liberty behind that cannon for them, and taking it all round, there was little sleep within the tepees.

The next morning I awoke early with hopefulness rising within my breast at the thought of again obtaining my liberty. The first sound I heard was the firing of cannon near at hand; it sounded beautiful; it was sweet music to my ears. Anticipating the prospect of seeing friends once more, I listened and breathed in the echo after every bomb.

The fighting commenced at seven o'clock by Gen. Strange's troops forcing the Indians to make a stand. It was continued until ten with indifferent success. The troops surely could not have known the demoralized condition of the Indians, else they would have compelled them to surrender. The fighting was very near, for the bullets were whizzing around all the time. We thought surely that liberty was not far away. The Indians were continually

"THE WANDERING SPIRIT."

riding back and fro inspiring their followers in the rear with hope, and we poor prisoners with despair. At last they came back and said that they had killed twenty policemen and not an Indian hurt. But there were two Indians killed, one of whom was the Worm, he who killed my poor husband, and several wounded. We were kept running and walking about all that morning with their squaws, keeping out of the way of their enemies, and our friends. We were taken through mud and water until my feet got so very sore that I could hardly walk at all.

The Indians ordered us to dig pits for our protection. Pritchard and Blondin dug a large one about five feet deep for us, and they piled flour sacks around it as a further protection ; but they dug it too deep and there was two or three inches of water at the bottom. They then threw down some brush and we got into it, twenty persons in all, with one blanket for Mrs. Delaney and me. McLean's family had another pit, and his daughters cut down trees to place around it. Mr. Mann and family dug a hole in the side of the hill and crawled into it. If I had my way I would have kept out of the pit altogether and watched my chance to escape.

We fully expected the troops to follow but they did not; and early in the morning we were up and off again. Some of the Indians went back to see how about the troops, and came back with the report that the " police " (they call all soldiers police) had vanished, they were afraid. When I heard it, I fairly sank, and the slight spark of hope I had, had almost gone out.   Just to think that succor was so near, yet alas! so far.   But for Mrs. Delaney I would have given way and allowed myself to perish.

CHAPTER XIV.

INDIAN BOYS.

JUST here a word about Indian boys would not be amiss. An Indian boy is a live, wild, and untamed being. He is full of mischief and cruelty to those he hates, and passably kind to those he likes. I never saw in their character anything that could be called love. They have no idea of such a tender tie. Thus by nature he is cruel without having a sense of humor, much less gayety, and in all my experience I never saw or heard one give a hearty laugh, except on the occasion of a mishap or accident to any one, and then the little fragment of humor is aroused.

He is skillful in drawing his bow and sling, and has a keenness of sight and hearing. He takes to the life of a hunter as a duck takes to water, and his delight is in shooting fowl and animals. He does it all with an ease and grace that is most astonishing. In everything of that nature he is very skillful. Pony riding is his great delight, when the ponies were not otherwise engaged, but during my stay with them, there was too much excitement and change all around for the boys to exercise that animal.

While we were driving along after breaking up camp the little fellows would run along and pick flowers for us, one vieing with the other as to who would get the most and the prettiest. They were gifted with a most remarkable memory and a slight was not very soon forgotten, while a kindness held the same place in their memory.

The general behaviour of Indian boys was nevertheless most intolerable to us white people. In the tepee there was no light and very often no fuel, and owing to the forced marches there was not much time for cutting wood, also it was hard to light as it was so green and sappy. The boys would then wrap themselves up in a blanket, but not to sleep, only to yell and sing as if to keep in the heat. They would keep this up until they finally dozed off; very often that would be in the early hours of the morning.

Like father, like son;. the virtues of young Indians were extremely few. They reach their tether when they fail to benefit self. Their morality was in a very low state. I do not remember that I saw much of it, if I did it was hardly noticible.

Where the charm of a savage life comes in I do not know, I failed to observe it during my experience in the camp of the Crees. The charm is a delusion, except perhaps when viewed from the deck of a steamer as it glided along the large rivers and lakes of the Indian country, or perhaps within the pages of a blood and thunder novel.

CHAPTER XV.

HOPE ALMOST DEFERRED.

ALMOST a week afterwards, on a Saturday night, the fighting Indians gathered around a tepee near ours and began that never ending dancing and singing. It was a most unusual thing for them to dance so close to our tent. They had never done so before. It betokened no good on their part and looked extremely suspicious. It seemed to me that they were there to fulfil the threat they made some time previous, that they would put an end to us soon. The hour was late and that made it all the more certain that our doom had come. I became very nervous and frightened at what was going on. When all at once there was a scattering, and running, and yelling at the top of their voices, looking for squaws and children, and tearing down tents, while we two sat in ours in the depths of despair, waiting for further developments. I clung to Mrs. Delaney like my own mother, not knowing what to do. The cause of the stampede we were told was that they had heard the report of a gun. That report was fortunate for us, as it was the intention of the Indians to wrench us from our half-breed protectors and kill us.

The tents were all down and in a very few minutes we were on the move again. It was Sunday morning at an early hour, raining heavily, and cold. We were compelled to travel all that day until eleven o'clock at night. The halt was only given then, because the brutes were tired themselves. Tents were pitched and comparative quietness reigned. Our bedding consisted of one blanket which was soaked with water. Andre Nault took pity on us and gave us his, and tried in every way to make us comfortable. I had a great aversion to that fellow; I was afraid to look at him. I was so weak and tired that I could not sleep but for only a few minutes. I had given up and despair had entered my mind. I told Mrs. Delaney I wished I could never see morning, as I had nothing to look forward to but certain death. In that frame of mind I passed the night.

CHAPTER XVI.

OUT OF BIG BEAR'S CAMP.

ONDAY morning, May 31st, was ushered in dark and gloomy, foggy and raining, but it proved to be the happiest day we had spent since the 31st of March.   As the night was passing, I felt its oppressiveness, I shuddered with the thought of what another day might bring forth ; but deliverance it seems was not far away ; it was even now at hand.   When the light of day had swallowed up the blackness of darkness, the first words that greeted my ears was Pritchard saying "I am going to watch my chance and get out of the camp of Big Bear." Oh ! what we suffered, Oh ! what we endured, during those two long months, as captives among a horde of semi-barbarians.   And to think that we would elude them, just when I was giving up in despair. It is said that the darkest hour is that which preceedes dawn ; weeping may endure for a night, but joy cometh in the morning.   So with me, in my utter prostration, in the act of giving way, God heard my prayer, and opened a way of deliverance, and we made the best of the opportunity.

> " No foe, no dangerous path we lead,
> Brook no delay, but onward speed."

Some of the Indians it seems had come across General Strange's scouts the night before, and in consequence, all kinds of rumors were afloat among the band.   They were all very much frightened, for it looked as if they were about to be surrounded.   So a move, and a quick one, was made by them, at an early hour, leaving the half-breeds to follow on.   This was now the golden opportunity, and Pritchard grasped it, and with him, five other half-breed families fled in an opposite direction, thereby severing our connection with the band nominally led by Big Bear.

We cut through the woods, making a road, dividing the thick brush, driving across creeks and over logs. On we sped. At one time hanging on by a corner of the bedding in order to keep from falling off the waggon. Another time I fell off the waggon while fording a stream; my back got so sore that I could not walk much. On we went roaming through the forest, not knowing where we were going, until the night of June 3rd the cry was made by Mrs. Pritchard with unfeigned disgust, "that the police were coming." Mrs. Delaney was making bannock for the next morning's meal, while I with cotton and crochet needle was making trimming for the dresses of Mrs. Pritchard's nine half-breed babies.

I threw the trimming work to the other end of the tent, and Mrs. Delaney called upon Mrs. Pritchard to finish making the bannocks herself, and we both rushed out just as the scouts galloped in.

THE HOME OF MR. AND MRS. J. A. GOWANLOCK.

CHAPTER XVII.

RESCUED.

RESCUED! at last, and from a life worse than death. I was so overjoyed that I sat down and cried. The rescuing party were members of General Strange's scouts, led by two friends of my late husband, William McKay and Peter Balentyne of Battleford. We were so glad to see them. They had provisions with them, and they asked us if we wanted anything to eat. We told them we had bannock and bacon, but partook of their canned beef and hard tack. It was clean and good; and was the first meal we enjoyed for two months.

I could not realize that I was safe until I reached Fort Pitt. The soldiers came out to welcome us back to life. The stories they heard about us were so terrible, that they could scarcely believe we were the same.

The steamer was in waiting to take us to Battleford. Rev. Mr. Gordon took my arm and led me on board. The same gentleman gave us hats, we had no covering for our heads for the entire two months we were captives We were very scant for clothing. Mrs. Delaney had a ragged print dress, while I managed to save one an Indian boy brought me while in camp. Upon reaching Battleford we were taken to the residence of Mr. Laurie.

Coming down on the steamer, on nearing a little island, we saw a number of squaws fishing and waving white flags. All along wherever we passed the Indians, they were carrying white flags as a token that they had washed off their war paint and desired rest.

CHAPTER XVIII.

WE LEAVE FOR HOME.

WE leave Battleford for Swift Current, and our journey takes us across the prairie; that same stretch that I travelled a few months before, but under different circumstances and associations. Then I went up as a happy bride, Now I go down *alone* and bowed with grief. Everything around is full of life, the prairie is a sea of green interpersed with beautiful flowers and plants. It is a pretty scene to feast upon, yet my soul cannot drink it in. I am on the way to friends, a feeling of desolation takes hold of me; but I must control myself, and by God's help I will, for his goodness is forever sure.

Rev. John McDougall, Dr. Hooper, Captain Dillon, Capt. Nash and Messrs. Fox and Bayley, of Toronto, and Mrs. Laurie accompanied us on the journey, and did everything they could to make us comfortable. The trip over the prairie was a pleasant one. When we got to the South Saskatchewan, a thunder storm came on which roughened the water so, we could not cross for about an hour. After it quieted down a scow came and carried us over. Friends there took care of us for the night, and on the 1st of July we boarded a train for Moose Jaw. Capt. Dillon on going to the post office met several young ladies in a carriage who asked where we were as they wished to take us to their homes for tea, he informed them that the train had only a few minutes to stop and that it would be impossible. Those same young ladies were back to the train before it started with a bottle of milk and a box full of eatables. At eleven o'clock p.m., we arrived at Regina, and remained with Mr. and Mrs. Fowler, going next morning to a hotel. We were there four days. At Moose Jaw we received the following kind letter from Mrs. C. F. Bennett, of Winnipeg:—

NEW DOUGLASS HOUSE, WINNIPEG, JUNE 8TH, 1885.

Mrs. Delaney and Mrs. Gowanlock:

DEAR MADAMS,—Although an entire stranger to both of you, I cannot resist the impulse to write you a few lines to say how thankful and delightful I am to hear of your rescue.

Before I was dressed this morning, my husband came up to tell me that you were both safe. And I cannot express to you, neither can you comprehend the joy that intelligence brought to *everyone*. The terrible stories of your being tortured and finally murdered, outraged the feelings of the whole civilized world, and while men swore to avenge your wrongs, women mourned you, as sisters.

I am very thankful to see by the papers that you were not so inhumanly treated as reported, although your experience has been a terrible one— and one which you can never forget.

I presume that as soon as you are a little rested, you will go east to your friends; should you do so, I will be most happy to entertain you while you are in Winnipeg.

After your captivity, you must be destitute of everything, and if you will come down here, we will be delighted to supply you with what you require. I do not know if you have personal friends here, or not, but your sufferings have given you a sister's place in every heart, and *every one* in Winnipeg would be deeply disappointed if you did not give them an opportunity of expressing their deep sympathy and regards.

Mr. Bennett unites with me in best wishes, and in hopes that you will accept our hospitality on your way east.

I am in deepest sympathy,

Sincerly yours,

MRS. C. F. BENNETT.

I shall never forget the words of sympathy that are expressed in this epistle, or the kindness of Mr. and Mrs. McCaul and the people of Winnipeg generally. On our way from Winnipeg to Parkdale we received every attention and assistance, which I can assure the reader went a long way in making sorrow lighter and more able to bear. I thank God for the sympathy that was extended to me by his people.   Mr. J. K. Macdonald of Toronto, was most assiduous in his attention to us from Winnipeg until we left the train at Parkdale on the 12th of July.   I must not forget the kindness of Mr. and Mrs. Armstrong also of Toronto, or the other ladies and gentlemen who were our fellow-passengers on the journey.

CHAPTER XIX

AT HOME.

HOME—torn from mine—back to the parental. I will now look back over the scene, taking a panoramic view of the whole, as it occurred from the day I left my father's house full of happiness and joy, until I entered it full of sorrow and suffering.

It is well for mankind that they are forbidden the knowledge of what will be their destiny. It was well-conceived by a loving father that it was for our interest to be kept in ignorance of what was in store, for we, his creatures. And thus it was that I entered upon the duties of the household, with a lightness of heart equal to that of any matron. In the humble home (I commence from there) in that beautiful north-west land of quietness and peace, there was not a ruffle heard, or a rumor sounded, of what was in store for that industrious little community. We were living in the bonds of fellowship with all mankind, and we had no fear. But in all that stillness there was an undercurrent at work that would soon make itself felt. Dissatisfaction on account of grievances, real or fancied, was blowing. It had broken out in one place, why should it not in another. This disaffected spirit was prevalent in all parts of that country. Who was to blame? who was the cause? direct or indirect, it is not my intention or desire to say; suffice it is to note, that there was discontent; and therefore there must have been grievances, and an attempt should have been made or an understanding arrived at, whereby this state of discontent should have been replaced by that of content, without disturbance. Where there is discontent there must be badness and suffering, with evils and excesses lying in its wake.

To have removed those grievances was the imperative
duty of the dispensers of law and order and thus avoid
those excesses, but it was not done in time and the inevitable
did come swift and sure ; the innocent were made to feel
its fury.   For that little hamlet by the creek was entered,
and its domestic quietness destroyed and future prospects
blighted.   There was a degree of uneasiness felt after we
were informed of the horror of Duck Lake.   Two half-
breeds, Blondin and Donaire, who were employed by my
husband, were observed in frequent and earnest conversation
with the Indians.   Those two had but arrived from the
scene at Duck Lake.   For what were they there?   Was it to
incite the Indians?   Their actions were, to say the least, suspicious.

I will not dwell on the terrible slaughter which followed,
it is too painful a subject, simply stating that I had not
believed that anything so awful would have been perpetrated
by either half-breeds or Indians, until we were taken out of
Mrs. Delaney's the second time, and then I felt that there
would be trouble, but not in such a manner as that.   When
I was dragged from the death-bed of my husband, who had
the ground for a couch and the canopy of heaven for a
coverlet, I was in a bewildered condition.   Half-unconsciously
I allowed the Indian to drag me on to his tepee, and once
in, the circumstances which led to my position, flitted through
my brain in quick succession.   I then realized that it was
most critical; in a few hours I would be forced to undergo
ill-treatment that would very soon kill me.   With those
thoughts within my mind, the tepee opened and a little girl
entered, an angel sent by God to be my deliverer.   Although
not aware, she was his instrument in taking me out of danger
and placing me in a purer atmosphere.   That child was
Pritchard's little girl and I asked her to send her father.   He
came and by his influence I was transferred to his care for a

while. And when I entered his tent and there saw Mrs. Delaney, I was overjoyed for a minute, and then all was a blank; the excitement proved too much for me and I swooned away. When I returned to consciousness they were all doing their best for me.

In a short time Blondin came in, (at the commencement of the massacre he left for our house) he brought with him our waggon, and oxen, and all the furniture and provisions he could take. Immediately thereafter the Indians appeared and it was then that he offered them $30 and a horse for our release. The offer was accepted and I was transferred to Blondin. The wretch was there with evil intent in his heart. I fully believe that he felt exultant over the doings of the day. Why did he go down to our house when that dreadful affair was going on? Why did he help himself to our goods? *Only* for a bad purpose. Oh! God I saw it all. He had everything arranged for me to live with him. All my husband's things; all my things; and a tent. But I refused to accept him or his conditions. I resented the infamous proposals as strongly as I was able, and appealed to John Pritchard for protection and he generously granted my request. I will never forget his kindness to me as long as I live: "Yes, Mrs. Gowanlock, you can share my tent, with myself and family, and I will protect you."

That dated the commencement of the shameful treatment I received at the hands of Blondin, and whenever Pritchard was absent, it was meted out to me to the full. Blondin purchased my liberty, that would have been a good action if prompted by honorable motives, but in the absence of that it has no weight with me. He was amply repaid, he got our oxen, our waggon, our provisions, our clothes, we had money there, perhaps he got that. I have wondered since was it not my money with which he purchased me. By the help of God I was saved from him ; and a life worse than death. If the worst had come I would have drowned or killed myself ; but it did not. "God moves in a mysterious way."

During the next two months I was called upon to witness heart-rending scenes; first the brutal treatment of the dead bodies of our husbands', as well as cruelty to ourselves; for even under Pritchard's care we were not safe and did not know what minute would be our last. Not content with murdering them in cold blood, they must needs perform diabolical deeds which causes me to shudder when I think of it. They danced around them with demoniac glee, kicking and pulling them in every direction, and we were the unwilling witnesses of such behaviour. And when we had them buried under the church they burned it down, with dancing and yelling, accompanied with hysterical laughter. The sight was sickening to me and I was glad they moved in the direction of Fort Pitt, leaving that place with all its associations of suffering and death. But when I heard that they intended to take the Fort, and destroy more life, I felt that I would rather remain where we were than witness any more scenes of so sad a nature. I have no happy tale to tell for this period was filled with woe and pain.

I will not enumerate further the trials I had to undergo day after day, but will pass rapidly on until the gladsome note was sounded by our hostess Mrs. Pritchard the "police are here." God delivered us again.

It is unnecessary to itemize in detail what passed from that time until I reached Ontario. I have told my tale, simple and truthful, and what remains for me now is my old home, my old associations, and my old life—the lines are hard to bear—" Thy will not mine be done."

> Once I thought my cross to heavy,
>   And my heart was sore afraid,
> Summoned forth to stand a witness
>   For the cause of truth betrayed.
>
> " Send, O Lord," I prayed, " some Simon,
>   As of old was sent to Thee."
> " Be a Simon," said the Master,
>   " For this cross belongs to me."
>
> Still is crucified my Saviour,
>   I myself must a Simon be;
> Take my cross and walk humbly
>   Up the slopes of Calvary.

TO ONE OF THE ABSENT.

You bade me good-bye with a smile, love,
  And away to the west wild and drear ;
At the sound of war's bugle shrill calling
  You went without shadow of fear.
But when I complained of your going,
  To face dangers untold in the west ;
You chided me gently by singing :
  " Encourage me dear 'twill be best."

" I know you will miss me each hour
  And grieve when I'm far, far away :
But its duty's demand and.I'm ready ;
  Could I show the white feather to-day ?
Oh ! Now, you're my own bright eyed blessing
  And show the true spirit within :
Those eyes now so fearlessly flashing
  Shall guide me through war's crash and din."

With your men you went cheerful and willing,
  To defend and take peace to the poor
Helpless children and sad prisoned women
  Who had homes on Saskatchewan's shore,
And now I'm so proud of you darling
  I can worship a hero so brave,
While I pray for your safe home returning ;
  When the peace flag shall quietly wave.

O'er the land where poor Scott's heartless mur-
    derer,
  Has added much more to his sin ;
By the cold-blooded uncalled for slaughter,
  Of Gowanlock, Delaney and Quinn,
Who like many others now sleeping,
  Shroudless near the sky of the west,
May be called the sad victims and martyrs
  Of Riel who's name we detest.

Many hearts are now mourning their lov'd ones
   Who died at their post, true and brave,
In defiance of one heartless rebel,
   Who's life not e'en "millions" should save.
So keep your arm strong for the fray dear,
   I'll not wish you back 'ere the fight
Shall decide for you, country and comrades,
   In favor of honour and right.

Let justice be done now unfailing
   Nought but *death* can atone for his sin ;
Let the fate he has meted to others ;
   By our dauntless be meted to him,
Don't return until quiet contentment ;
   Fills the homes now deserted out west,
And the true ring of peace finds an echo,
   In each sturdy settler's breast.

And when you are homeward returning,
   With heart that has never known fear ;
Remember the love light is burning,
   Unceasingly, constantly, here
And " Bright Eyes " will give you a welcome
   Which even a soldier may prize
While the lips will be smiling with pleasure,
   That have prayed in your absence with sighs.

And the whole world shall ring with the praises
   Of Canada's noblest and best ;
Who shoulder to shoulder defended,
   And saved the unhappy North-West
While in coming years 'round the hearthstone
   Will be told how the dark coats and red,
Put to rout Riel, rebels and half-breeds
   And aveng'd both the living and dead.

CLEOMATI.

·20 Alexander St., Toronto.

SHOT DOWN.

THEY died a brutal death on the 2nd of April, disarmed first, and then shot down. The perpetrators of that outrage were actuated by fiendish instincts, nevertheless they had an intuition of what was meant by civilization. How they could have so forgotten the training they had received religiously and socially to have allowed the lower instincts of the savage to gain the ascendancy and fell in cold blood—not extortioners or land-grabbers—but their spiritual advisers ; their superintendent ; their farm instructor, and those who had left comfortable homes in the east in order to carry civilization into the remote places of the west. The work that they were performing was calculated to elevate the Indian and make him a better man ; taking him from his miserable mode of living and leading him into a more happy and prosperous life for this and the next. It is unaccountable, and there is yet a something that will come to the surface that was the real cause for this dreadful act. At this point a brief sketch of the lives of some of those killed would not be out of place

They numbered nine, the entire male population of that growing little village. There were T. Quinn, J. Delanay, J. A. Gowanlock, T. Dill, W. C. Gilchrist, J. Williscraft, C. Gouin and Father Fafard and a priest from Onion Lake. Mr. Quinn was the Indian agent for that district well fitted in every particular for the position he held. Mr. Dill kept a general store and at one time lived at Bracebridge, was a brother of the member of Muskoka in the local house. Mr. Williscraft came from Owen Sound where his friends reside. C. Gouin was a native of the north-west.

MR. GOWANLOCK.

JOHN ALEXANDER GOWANLOCK, one of the Frog Lake martyrs, was born in the City of Stratford, Province of Ontario, on the 17th of April, 1861. He was the youngest son of Mr. Jas. Gowanlock, of East Otto, Cattaraguas County, New York State. He has three brothers living, and one sister, A. G. and J. Gowanlock of Parkdale, Ontario, R. K. Gowanlock, of Oscoda, Michigan, and Mrs. Daisy Huntsman, of Tintern, Co. Lincoln. From a boy he was a general favorite, quiet and unassuming, yet withal, firm and decided in his opinions. After leaving Stratford he resided for some time in Barrie, and then went to the Village of Parkdale, where he resided until he left for the north-west.

Being in ill-health (at the age of 19), his physician and aunt, Dr. J. K. Trout, of Toronto, advised a change of climate, and acting upon that advice left for that great country. After a short residence every symptom of disease had vanished, and upon his return some eighteen months after, he felt and was a new man in every particular. In three months time he returned to the land of his adoption. By honesty and energy he succeeded well. He took hold of every kind of work that he thought would pay. He became farmer, mill-builder, speculator, surveyor, store-keeper and mill-owner in succession, buying and selling, and at the same time pushing further west. His greatest success was in Battleford, the Indians of that district would flock to his store, because they knew they could get a good article at a reasonable price. Last year the Government wanted mills for the

MR. GOWANLOCK.

reserves in the region of Frog Lake, and after negotiating with them for some time he finally decided, in conjunction with Mr. Laurie, to accept the offer made, the Government giving them the sum of $2,800 as an inducement.

In the month of October of last year, he began operations, which, if those poor, deluded savages, who did not know when they were well off, had allowed him to finish, would long ere this been a hive of industry and a blessing to those Indians. He visited Ontario the same year, buying all the machinery necessary for the mills and superintending its shipment. He also took unto himself a wife from among the fair daughters of Ontario, and never a happier couple went forth to brave the cares of life. Both young and full of energy.

But they were not allowed to enjoy their domestic bliss long. The sad event which terminated with him being murdered, along with eight others, being still fresh in the memory of all; it was a sudden call, but he was prepared for it. An oath was never uttered by him, nor did he know the taste of liquor, a temperance man in the full meaning of the term. He also took a hearty interest in church matters having been one of the managers of the Battleford Presbyterian Church. Wherever he went he did good, in a gentle and kind way; and he will be remembered by both Indian, half-breed and settler, as one who never took advantage of them in any way, and the very soul of honor.

> Not himself, but the truth that in life he had spoken,
> Not himself, but the seed that in life he had sown,
> Shall pass to the ages—all about him forgotten,
> Save the truth he had spoken, the things he had done.

MR. GILCHRIST.

MR. GILCHRIST.

ONE of the victims of the Frog Lake massacre was William Campbell Gilchrist, a native of the village of Woodville, Ontario, and eldest son of Mr. J. C. Gilchrist, Postmaster of that place. He was an energetic young man, of good address, and if spared would have made his mark in the land of promise. Prior to going there, he held situations in various parts of this province, and they were all of such a nature, as to make him proficient in the calling of his adoption, he had splendid business ability and with a good education, made progress that was quite remarkable for one of his years, at the time of his murder he was only in his twenty-fourth year.

He was clerk for Mr. E. McTavish of Lindsay, for some time; he then returned to his home to take a situation which had been offered him by Mr. L. H. Staples, as assistant in his general store ; he afterwards went to the village of Brechin as Clerk and Telegraph Operator, for Messrs. Gregg & Todd. While there he formed the acquaintance of Mr. A. G. Cavana, a Surveyor, and it was through his representations that he directed his steps to the great unknown land. Shortly after his acquaintance with Mr. Cavana, that gentleman received a government appointment as surveyor in the territories, taking Mr. Gilchrist with him in the capacity of book keeper and assistant surveyor ; they left in the spring of 1882. He was well fitted for the position, for besides being an excellent penman, was an expert at figures ; when the winter set in, he remained there, taking a situation in a store in Winnipeg, and when the summer opened out he again went with Mr. Cavana on the survey, (1883) on his way home in the autumn he fell in with Mr. J. A. Gowan-lock, who induced him to remain with him as clerk, with whom he never left until that sad morning on the 2nd of April, when he was shot down in his strength and manhood. He was a member of the Presbyterian church having confessed at the early age of 14 years. It was his intention to enter the Manitoba College as a theological student.

DEDICATED

TO

OUR SISTERS.

THE

LADIES OF CANADA.

A WAR DANCE AT FORT PITT.

Two Months

—in the—

Camp of Big Bear.

The Life and Adventures

OF

Theresa Gowanlock and Theresa Delaney.

PART II.

PARKDALE:

TIMES OFFICE, 24 QUEEN STREET

1885.

MRS. DELANEY.

PREFACE.

EVERAL friends have asked me to write a sketch of my life and more especially of my adventures in the North-West. At first I hesitated before promising to comply with the request. There is a certain class of orators who, invariable, commence their public address by stating that they are "unaccustomed to public speaking." It may be true in many cases, but most certainly no public speaker was ever less accustomed to address an audience, than I am to write a book. Outside my limited correspondence, I never undertook to compose a page, much less a book. But, if any excuse were necessary, I feel that the kindness of the people I have met, the friendliness of all with whom I have come in contact, during the last eventful half-year, would render such excuse uncalled for. I look upon the writing of these pages as a duty imposed upon me by gratitude. When memory recalls the sad scenes through which I have passed, the feeling may be painful, but there is a pleasure in knowing that sympathy has poured a balm upon the deep wounds, and that kindness and friendship have sweetened many a bitter drop in the cup of my sorrrow and trouble.

"There is a tide in the affairs of men," sang England's great Bard, but we never know when it is about to turn, or if that turn will be the ebb or the flow of happiness. "The veil of the Future is woven by the hand of Mercy." Could I have but caught a glimpse through its folds, some three years ago, I might not have the story to tell that you, kind reader, will find in this short work. I might not be, to-day, mourning the loss of a dear husband.

But who can judge of the ways of Divine Providence ? For His own wise ends has the Almighty permitted such things to take place : and submissive to His will, I feel that instead of repining, I should return Him thanks for my own life and preservation ; and, under God, I must thank my friends one and all !

If this little sketch should prove instructive or even interesting to anyone I will feel doubly repaid. The scenes I have to describe, the story I have to tell, would require the pen of a Fenimore Cooper to do them justice. Feeling myself unable to relate all I experienced and suffered, in an adequate manner, I will merely offer the public, a simple, truthful, unvarnished tale and for every fact thereof, I give my word that it is no fiction, but real truth.

With this short preface I will now crave the indulgence of my readers, while they peruse the following pages.

THERESA DELANEY.

Two Months in the Camp of Big Bear.

MRS. DELANEY.

CHAPTER I.

MY YOUTH AND EARLY LIFE.

AS the principal object of this work, is to give an account of my experiences in the North-West, and my many adventures during the last few months, I would deem it out of place to detain my readers with any lengthy description of my birth-place or any details of my younger days. I have noticed many false reports that have been circulated through the press, upon the different situations and conditions in the North-West—whether as to the whites, the half-breeds, or the Indians. In the second chapter I will give a truthful version of what I saw, heard and know. Still I cannot well enter upon this work, with justice to myself or to my late husband, without informing my readers whence we came and how our lots happened to be cast together amidst the scenes of our new home, and upon the theatre of the fearful tragedy in which we played such important parts.

My grandfather, Henry Marshall Fulford, while yet a young man, about the year 1812, came from Woburn Massachusetts, and established his home on the Aylmer road, near Bytown, the Ottawa of to-day, where he carried on an extensive lumbering and farming business. My father was born there, and it was also the place of my own birth. Our home was situated about two miles and a half from Aylmer, and about five miles from the present capital of the Dominion.

In those days Ottawa was called Bytown.   No one then dreamed that it was destined to become the capital and the seat of the future Federal government of the country.   The town, for it was then a town, was small and far from attractive, and the surrounding country was not very much inhabited.   The lumbering operations constituted the staple commerce, and the shanties were the winter homes of the greater number of the people.

Nearly all my life, except the last three years, was spent at home.   I never travelled much, and in fact, never expected to become a traveller, and above all, an unwilling heroine in the North-West troubles.   I had several sisters and brothers.   I was the eldest of the family, and as such, for many years had to devote my time to household cares.   My school-days s em now the pleasantest period of my early life.   Since then I have known many ups and downs ; but never felt the same peace of mind and gayness of spirit that I have felt in days now gone.   I might say that I have lived three distinct l ves.   From my birth until the day of my marriage, which took place on the 27th of July, 1882, I led a uniform life.   Few, if any changes, marked each passing year.   The seasons came and went, and the winter's snow fell and the summer's sun ripened the golden harvests, and days flowed into weeks, weeks into months, months into years, and year succeeded year as I felt myself growing into womanhood.   The changes in my life were few and my troubles so small, that memory had scarcely ever to recall a dark or dreary scene and hope always beckoned me on to the future.

The only events that seemed to stand out, landmarks in the past, were two deaths in the family—the first my eldest brother and the second my dearly beloved and much lamented father.

Had it not been for these two events I might drop a veil

over all the past and consider merely that I had lived through such a number of years :—these years, like the great desert of the east, would stretch back, an unbroken tract, with no object to break the monotony of the scene. But, as the kirches tombs or monuments of Arabia, rise up in solemn grandeur from out the lonliness of the plain, casting their shadows of the sandy waste, so these two monuments or tombs appear upon the level scene of my uneventful past. Could I, then, have caught one glimpse adown the valley of the "Yet to be," what a different picture would have presented itself to my vision ! A confusion of adventures, a panorama never ending, ever shifting, of an eventful life.

My second life might be called a period from my wedding day until the 2nd of April, 1885. And the third, the last and most eventful life, is that of three months—April, May and June, 1885. To the second important period in my career I will consecrate the next chapter and to the third and final part of my life will be devoted the last chapter.

My husband was born in Napean, in the Province of Ontario, about the end of 1846. Physically speaking, he was a man of very fine appearance. Over six feet in height and weighing about two hundred and ten pounds. His youth was spent in his native place, where he went to school and where he commenced his life of labor and exertion. I don't know, exactly, when it was that I first met him ; but I must have been quite young, for I remember him these many years. He was, during the last ten years that he lived in the Ottawa valley, foreman for diflerent lumber firms. Naturally gifted to command, he knew the great duty of obedience, and this knowledge raised him in the estimation of all those whose business he undertook to direct. And owing to that good opinion, he received a general recommendation to the government, and in the year 1879, he was appointed Indian instructor for the north-west.

Like my own life, his was uneventful. Outside the circle of his friends—and that circle was large—he was unknown to the public. Nor was he one of those who ever sought notoriety. His disposition was the very opposite of a boastful one.

Often I heard tell of the north-west. But I never took any particular interest in the country previous to his appointment and departure for his new sphere. I knew by the map, that such a region existed—just as I knew that there was a Brazil in South America, or a vast desert in the centre of Africa. Our statesmen were then forming plans to build the great Pacific Road, that band of iron which was soon destined to unite ocean to ocean. However, I never dreamed that I would one day visit those vast regions, the former home of the buffalo, the haunt of the prairie-chicken and the prairie-wolf. It never dawned upon me, that as I watched the puffing of the engine that rushed along the opposite side of the Ottawa from my home, that, one day, I would go from end to end of that line,—pass over those vast plains and behold the sun set, amidst the low poplars of the rolling prairies,—listen to the snort of the same engine as it died away, in echo, amongst the gorges of the Rockies. My husband had been three years, previous to our marriage, in the north west. His first winter was spent at "Onion Lake," there being no buildings at "Frog Lake." In fact, when he arrived there, "Frog Lake" district was a wilderness. During those three years I began to take some interest in that "land of the setting sun,"—but, as yet, I scarcely imagined that I would ever see the places he described. In 1882, my husband returned to Ottawa and his principal object in coming, was to take me, as his wife, away with him to his new home.

We were married in Aylmer on the 27th July, 1882. Our intention was to start for the wilds on the first day of August.   In the next chapter I will take up that second period of my life and strive to describe our trip and what we saw, learned and experienced during the following three years.

My readers will have to excuse what may seem egotism on my part, in speaking so much about myself and my husband.   But as the subject demands that I should detail, all that can be of any public interest, in my short life, it would be difficult to write my story and not appear, at times, somewhat egotistical.

This first chapter must necessarily be short, when one has ñothing to write about it is hard to fill up pages, and my life, and that of my husband, so far as I know, were most uneventful up to the day of our union, when

> "We joined the hands of each other,
>   To move through the stillness and noise
> *Dividing* the *cares* of existence,
>   But *doubling* its *hopes* and its *joys*."

My younger days seem to have passed away like a quiet dream, leaving but a faint memory behind ; but my last period of life resembles more some frightful night-mare and I often wonder can it be true that I have passed through such scenes or is the whole affair a fevered vision of the night !

Now that I am safely home again with my good dear mother beside me, my fond brothers and sisters around me, it would appear as if I had never got married, never left them, never saw the north-west, never suffered the exposure, loss, sorrow, turmoil, dangers and terrors of the late rebellion. But fancy cannot destroy the truth—the real exists in spite of the ideal, and, as I enter upon my description, faint and imperfect as it may be, I feel my hand shake with nervous excitement, my pulse throb faster, my heart beat heavier, as scene after scene of the great drama passes before me, clear and perfect as when first enacted.   Had I only the language at my command, as I have the pictures before me, at my summons—I feel that I could do justice to the subject. But as I was never destined to be an authoress and my powers of composition were dealt out to me with a sparing hand, I can but express my regret that an abler writer does not hold my pen. A cloud has come over my life-dream. The angel of death passed by and in the shadow of his wing a heavy and better stroke was dealt. It may not be of much interest to the pnblic to know how I feel over my loss, but if each one would, for a moment, suppose the case their own and then reflect upon what the feeling must be. Let them attempt to write a cold, matter-of-fact statement of the events, to detail them simply as they took place, without giving expression to sentiments of sorrow, I think that, at least, ninety-nine out of every hundred would fail, and the one who could succeed would appear, in my mind, a person without heart or feeling, unable to love and unworthy of affection.

I will strive to push on to the end of my undertaking without tiring my readers, with vain expressions of sorrow, regret or pain; but do not expect that I can relate the story from first to last, without giving vent to my feelings.

There is one pleasure, however, in knowing that I have no complaints to make, no blame to impute, no bitter feelings to arouse, no harsh words to say. But on the contrary, I will try not to forget the kindness, sympathy, and protection, that from one source or another were tendered to me.

I hope this little book will please all who read it; amuse some; instruct others; but I pray sincerely that not one of all my readers may ever be placed in the painful situation through which I have passed. Methinks some good prayers have gone up to heaven for me, and that the Almighty lent an attentive ear to the supplications; for like the angel that walked through the flaming furnace to protect the just men of old, some spirit of good must have stood by my side to guide me in safety through the fiery ordeal and to conduct me to that long wished for haven of rest—my old home on the Aylmer Road.

MR. DELANEY.

CHAPTER II.

MY MARRIAGE LIFE.

M Y wedding took place in the usual manner; the same congratulations, presents, kisses, well-wishes all the world over. I need not dwell upon the event any further.

On the 1st August, L882, my husband took the train at Ottawa, *en route* for the North-West. As far as the first portion of our trip is concerned I have little or nothing to say, I could not see much from the car window and every place was new to me and, in fact, one place seemed as important as another in my eyes.

We passed through Toronto and thence to Sarnia, and on to Chicago. We crossed to Port Huron and proceeded at once to St. Paul. This was our first stoppage. We spent a day in St. Paul, and, indeed, the city deserves a day, at least, from all who travel that way. It is a beautiful place. However, it seemed to me much on the same plan and in the same style as all the Western American cities. From St. Paul's we went on to Winnipeg. I must say that I was not very favourably impressed by my first visit to this metropolis of the North-West. On my homeward trip I found vast changes for the better in the place. Still it may have been only to my eye that the city appeared far from clean and anything but attractive. I must admit that it was rainy weather—and oh ! the mud ! I have heard that there are two classes of people leave Quebec after a first visit—the one class are those who caught a first glimpse of the Rock City on a beautiful day. These people are unceasing in their admiration of Quebec. The other class are those, who came into the city, for the first time, on a rainy day, when the streets were canals and mud was ankle deep. It would be impossible to convince these people that Quebec was anything but a filthy, hilly, crooked, ugly, unhealthy place. I may be of the latter class, when I refer to Winnipeg. But most assuredly I am not prejudiced, for since my last passage through that city I have changed my idea of it completely.

From Winnipeg we proceeded by rail to Brandon and thence, by construction train, to Troy. We were then four hundred miles from Winnipeg and we had four hundred miles to travel. But our cars ceased here. At Troy we got our tent ready, supplied ourselves with the necessaries upon such a journey, and getting our buckboard into order, we started upon the last, the longest and yet pleasantest part of our voyage.

How will I attempt to describe it! There is so much to tell and yet I know not what is best to record and what is best to leave out.

Half a day's journey from Troy we crossed the Qu'Appelle river. The scenery upon the banks of that most picturesque of streams would demand the pencil of a Claude Lorraine, or the pen of a Washington Irving to do it justice. Such hills I never before beheld. Not altogether for size but for beauty. Clad in a garb of the deepest green they towered aloft, like the battlement of two rival fortresses—and while the sun lit up the hills to our right, the shades of mid-day deepened upon the frowning buttresses to our left. Every tree seemed to have a peculiar hue, a certain depth of color completely its own. Indeed, one would imagine that Dame Nature had been trying a gigantic crazy quilt and had flung it over the bed of the Qu'Appelle valley, that all who went by might admire her handiwork.

I might here remark that the days of the summer are longer, in the north-west, than in the Ottawa district.   In fact, we used to rise at three o'clock in the morning and drive for three hours before our breakfast.   It would then be grey dawn and the flush of approaching day-light could be seen over the eastern hills.   At nine o'clock in the evening it would be twilight.   The days of midwinter are proportionately shorter.

The road we had to travel was a lovely one; at times it might be a little rough, but indeed it could well compare with most of the roads in our more civilized places.   Nearly every night we managed to reach a clump of bushes or shelter to camp.   Except for two days, when on the "Salt Plains," when like the caravans in the deserts of the east we had to carry our own fuel and water.

We crossed the South Saskatchewan at Aroline—or the "Telegraph Crossing," also known as Clark's Ferry—from the man who kept the ferry, and who made the new trail running to the Touchwood Hills.   We again crossed the the North Saskatchewan near Fort Pitt—which is thirty-five miles from our destination.

We went by the river road, and after we crossed the salt plains, and got into the woods at Eagle Creek, we had a splendid trip through a rich fertile abundant farming country.   The houses are not very attractive, but the farms are really fine.   I will dwell upon this question at a greater length presently.

That less confusion may take place, I will sub-divide this chapter into three sections.   In the first I will speak of the farms and farmers—their homes and how they live; in the second, I will describe our own home and its surroundings; and in the third, I will speak of the Indians under my husband's control, and tell how we got along during the three years I was there.

THE FARMERS AND THEIR FARMS.

It would be out of place and even impossiby for me, at present to give you any figures relating to the crops and harvests of the North-West. Suffice, to say that for two summers, at Frog Lake, in my husband's district, we raised wheat that was pronounced by competent judges to equal the best that ever grew in Ontario.

The land is fertile and essentially a grain-bearing soil. It is easy to clear, and is comparatively very level. There is ample opportunity to utilize miles upon miles of it, and the farms that exist, at present, are evidences of what others might be. No one can tell the number of people that there is room for in the country. Europe's millions might emigrate and spread themselves over that immense territory, and still there would be land and ample place for those of future generations. We were eight hundred miles from Winnipeg, and even at that great distance we were, to use the words of Lord Dufferin, "only in the anti-chamber of the great North-West."

The country has been well described by hundreds, it has also been falsely reported upon by thousands. At first it was the "Great Lone Land,"—the country of bleak winter, eternal snow and fearful blizzards. Then it became a little better known, and, suddenly it dawned upon the world that a great country lie sleeping in the arms of nature, and awaiting the call of civilization to awaken it up and send it forth on a mission of importance. The "boom" began. All thoughts were directed to the land of the Rockies. Pictures of plenty and abundance floated before the vision of many thousands. Homes in the east were abandoned to rush into the wilds of the West. No gold fever of the South was ever more exciting, and to add thereto, they found that the government proposed building a line of railway from end to end of the

Dominion.   Then the Frazer, Saskatchewan, Red River and
Assiniboine became household words.

In this story of a fancied land of plenty, there was much
truth, but as in every case in life, there was much falsehood
as well.   It suited the purpose of monied speculators to laud
to the skies the North-west in general.   But rich and extensive as the land may be, no man can expect to make a fortune there, unless through hard labor, never ceasing exertion
and great watchfulness.   There, as in all other lands, you
must "earn your bread by the sweat of your brow."   That
sentence passed on man, when the first sin darkened his
soul, shall exist and be carried into execution unto the end
of time.   And no man is exempt, and no land is free from
it.   Many have failed in finding riches in the North-West ;
gold did not glitter along the highway, nor were precious
stones to be picked up in every foot path.   The reason is,
because they went there expecting to have no work to do,
merely to sit down, to go to bed, to sleep and wake up some
morning millionaires.   But those who put their shoulder to
the wheel and their hands to the plough, turned up as rich a
soil as England's flag floats over, and sowed seeds that gave
returns as plentiful as the most abundant harvests on the
continent.   It would do one good to drive along the river
road by the Saskatchewan, and observe those elegant, level,
fertile, well tilled farms that dot the country.   It is a great
distance to procure materials for building, and as yet the
most of the houses are rough and small, but comfortable
and warm, and sufficient for the needs of the farmers.

Much of the labor is done in the old style, as in my own
native place, before the days of machinery.   But soon we
will see the mower and reaper finding their way into the very
furthest settlements—and if ever there was a country laid
out for the use of machinery it is certainly the north-west.

Before many years, there will be good markets for the produce, as the towns are growing up pretty rapidly and the railroad is lending a great encouragement to the farmers near the line.

Half a century ago the country was unheard of, save through the Hudson Bay Company's agents and factors: quarter of a century ago it was considered a *probably* future portion of our Dominion. Behold it to-day! Its cities, its roads, its villages, its farms, its inhabitants! What then may the immense territory not become before fifty years more shall have rolled into eternity? I do not feel myself competent to judge—but I have no doubt but it will become the grainery of the continent and the supplier of half Europe.

The farmer in the Provinces who has a good farm and who can make a fair living would be foolish to leave it for the hazard of an attempt in the new country. But should a person be commencing life and have the intention of depending upon themselves, their own exertion and energy, then the sun shines not on a finer land, holding out a broader prospect than in that great country that lies towards the Pacific.

I have only spoken hurriedly and from a general standpoint of the farmers, and when I say farmers, I mean white people. The Indian farming is of a different nature altogether. That will demand my attention before I close this chapter.

FROG LAKE AND SURROUNDINGS.

Although the name of the place would indicate that the lake abounded in frogs, still I have no recollection of seeing any extra number of them around the place. I think the name comes from a tradition—perhaps in some age, long lost in the twilight of Indian story, the frogs may have been more plentiful in that special locality than elsewhere. Twenty miles from our farm and twelve miles from Fort

Pitt is "Onion Lake" farm, where my husband spent his first winter. I cannot tell how that place got its name no more than how our district was called *Aieekesegahagan*. When I first arrived at Frog Lake there were no buildings excepting my husband's house and warehouse—a shed and garden, added thereto, formed the whole establishment. These were built by my husband. Since then, in the course of three years that I was there, several buildings were put up, until, in fine, our little settlement became quite a village.

Mr. Quinn's, (the agent) house, and his storehouse, were erected since I arrived there. Mr. Quinn was the gentleman whose name has appeared so much in the public prints since the sad events of the second of April last. When I come to my experience during the last three months of my North-West life, I will give more fully the story of Mr. Quinn's fate. There were three reserves near us, the Indians upon which were under my husband's control—In the next section of this chapter I will refer to these bands and give what I know about them.

The scenery around Frog Lake is surpassingly beautiful. We lived on Frog Creek, which runs from the Lake into the North Saskatchewan. In October last, Mr. Gowanlock, who shared the same fate as my husband, and whose kind and gentle wife was my companion through all the troubles and exposures of our captivity and escape, began to build a mill two miles from our place, on the waters of Frog Creek. He put up a saw mill and had all the timber ready to complete a grist mill, when he was cut short in his early life, and his wife was cast upon the mercy of Providence. They lived two miles from us. Many of those whom I knew were mill hands. Gilchrist who was killed, was an employee of Mr. Gowanlock.

Frog Lake is pretty large. I know that in one direction

it is twelve miles long.   In the centre of the lake is a large island, that is clothed in a garb of evergreen.   The pine and spruce upon it are extra large, sound and plentiful.   In fact it would be difficult to find a place where better timber for building and other purposes, could be cut.   The place is gradually becoming developed, and when I consider all that has been done, in the way of improvement, since I first went there, I would not be snrprised to learn, that in the near future, the principal parts of the country shall be under cultivation, that the clang of the mill shall be heard upon every stream, and that down the Saskatchewan may float the produce of a fresh, a virgin, a teeming soil, to supply the markets of the Old World, and to supplant the over-worked fields of the eastern countries.

Also since my arrival at the Frog Lake Reserve, the priest's house, the school house and church were built.   Even there in the far west, away so to speak, from the atmosphere of civilization, beyond the confines of society, we have what Sir Alexander Selkirk mourned for so much, when alone on Juan Fernandez—*Religion*.   Even there, the ministers of the Gospel, faithful to their duties, and mindful of the great command to "go forth and teach all nations,"—leaving their homes and friends in the land of the east, seek out the children of those Indian tribes, and bring to them the lights of faith and instruction.   Untiring in their exertions, indefatigable in their labors, they set a glorious example, and perform prodigies of good.   The church was small, but neat, and although its ornaments are few, still I am sure that as fervent and as acceptable prayers went up, like incense, towards heaven, and blessings as choice, like dew, fell upon the humble worshippers, as ever the peal of the cathedral organ announced, or as ever decended upon the faithful beneath the gorgeous domes of the most splendid Basilicas. Memory still oftens summons up before me the scenes of silent, dusky, faithful children of the forest, kneeling in prayer, and with mingled feelings of awe, wonder, admiration and confidence, listening to the divine truths as explained in their own language, by the missionaries. But the picture becomes dark when I reflect upon the fate of the two good men whose sad story I have yet to tell. Most assuredly theirs was a *confession of blood*—and dying at their posts, faithful to their mission, relieving the soul of an expiring christian when the hand of death fell upon them. Theirs must have been a triumphal entry into heaven, to the kingdom of God! The great cross that the 90th Battalion placed over the united graves of the victims of the Frog Lake massacre, is a fitting emblem and a worthy monument; its base rests upon the soil that covers their union in the grave, but its summits points to where their souls are united above.

I will now take up the question of the Indians under my husband's control, and I will tell how they got along, improved, and were contented and happy. That will bring me to my last and all important chapter—the one which will contain the story so tragically mournful.

THE INDIANS AS THEY ARE

It would not become me, perhaps, to comment upon the manner in which the country is governed, and the Indians instructed, for I am no politician. In fact I dont know one party from another except by name. But I cannot permit this occasion, the last I may ever have, to go past without saying plainly what I think and what I know about the north-west and its troubles.

The half-breeds, or whites or others may have real or imaginary grievances that they desire to see redressed. If they have, I know nothing about them; I never had anything to do with them and maybe I could not understand the nature of their claims, even if explained to me. But be that as it may—even if I did know aught I would not feel myself justified in writing down that which I could only have learned by hear say.   But there is one thing I do know and most emphatically desire to express and have thoroughly understood and that is the fact *the Indians have no grievances and no complaints to make*.   Their treatment is of the best and most generous kind.   The government spares no pains to attempt to make them adopt an agricultural life, to teach them to rely upon their own strength, to become independent people and good citizens.   Of the Indians I can speak openly for I know them thoroughly.   There may be, here and there, a bad man amongst them ; but as a people they are submissive, kind, and, if only from curiosity, they are anxious to learn.   My husband remarked that according as they advanced in their agricultural knowledge that they commenced to have a liking for it.   And I noticed the same in the young squaws whom I undertook to instruct in household duties.

Many an English, Scotch or Irish farmer, when he comes poor to Canada and strives to take up a little farm for himself, if he had only one half the advantages that the government affords to the Indians, he would consider his fortune forever made.   They need never want for food.   Their rations are most regularly dealt out to them and they are paid to clear and cultivate their own land.   They work for themselves and are, moreover, paid to do so—and should a crop fail they are certain of their food, anyway.   I ask if a man could reasonably expect more ?   Is it not then unjust to lead these poor people into a trouble which can but injure them deeply !   If half-breeds have grievances let them get them redressed if they chose, but let them not mix up the Indians in their troubles.   The Indians have nothing to complain of and as a race they are happy in their quite home of the wilderness and I consider it a great shame for evil-

minded people, whether whites or half-breeds, to instill into
their excitable heads the false idea that they are presecuted
by the government. In speaking thus I refer to *our* Indians
that is to say those under my late husband's control. But
if all government agencies and reserves are like that at
Frog Lake, I hesitate not to say, that the government is
over good to the restless bands of the west.

I have no intention in my sketch to use any names—for
if I mention one of my friends I should mention them all
and that would be almost impossible. No more will I mention the names of any persons who might be implicated in
the strange and dishonest acts that have taken place previous to, during and since the outbreak. Yet I feel it a duty
to present a true picture of the situation of the Indian bands
and of the two great powers that govern in the country and
whose interests are the very opposite of each other.

These two governing parties are the Hudson Bay Company and the Dominion Government. There is not the
slightest doubt, but their interests are directly opposed. The
company has made its millions out of the fur trade and its
present support is the same trade. The more the Indians
hunt the more the Company can make. Now the Government desires to civilize them and to teach them to cultivate
the soil. The more the Indian works on his farm the less
the Company gets in the way of fur. Again, the more the
Government supplies the Indians with rations the less the
Company can sell to them.

Two buffalos are not given for a glass of whiskey—one-
third highwines and two-thirds water—as when the Company
had full sway. The fire-water is not permitted to be brought
to them now. No longer have the Indians to pay the ex-
orbitant prices for pork, flour, tea, &c., that the Company
charged them. The Government has rendered it unnecessary for them to thus sacrifice their time and means. Did

the Company ever try to civilize or christianize the Indians!
Most certainly not.   The more they became enlightened the
less hold the Company would have upon them.   Again, if
it were not for the Government, the lights of the gospel would
scarcely ever reach them.   The more the Government civi-
lizes them and developes the country, the less plentiful the
the game becomes, and the less profit the Company can
make.   Therefore it is that I say, the interests of the Company and those of tne Government are contradictory.   The
former wants no civilization, plenty of game, and Indians
that will hunt all the year around.   The latter require agri-
culture, the soil to be taken from the wild state, the rays of
faith and instruction to penetrate the furthest recess of the
land, and to have a race that can become worthy of the
diginity of citizens in a civilized country.   So much the worse
for the Government if the Indians rebel and so much the
worse for the Indians themselves ; but so much the better
for the Company's interests.

I have my own private opinions upon the causes of the
rebellion but do not deem it well or proper to express
them.   There are others besides the half-breeds and Big
Bear and his men connected with the affair.   There are
many objects to be gained by such means and there is a
"wheel within a wheel" in the North-West troubles.

As far as I can judge of the Indian character, they are
not, at all, an agricultural people—nor for a few generations
are they likely to become such.   Their habits are formed,
their lives are directed in a certain line—like a sapling you
can bend at will and when grown into a tree you cán no
longer change its shape—so with them.   From time immemorial they have ranged the woods and it is not in the
present nor even the next generation that you can uproot
that inclination.   Take the negro from the south and place
him amongst the ice-bergs of the arctic circle and strive to

make him accustomed to the hunting of the seal or harpooning of the walruss ;—or else bring down an Esquimaux and put him into a sugar-cane plantation of the topics.   In fact, take a thorough going farmer from the old-country and attempt to accustom him to hunt moose and trap beaver. He may get expert at it ; but give him a chance and he will soon fling away the traps and pick up the spade, lay down the rifle and take hold of the plough.   So it is with the Indians—they may get a taste for farming, but they prefer to hunt.   Even the best amongst them had to have a month every spring and another month every fall to hunt.   And they would count the weeks and look as anxiously forward to those few days of freedom, of unbridled liberty, as a school-boy looks forward to his mid-summer holidays.

Yet, in spite of this hankering after the woods and the freedom of the chase, they are a people easily instructed, quick to learn, (when they like to do so), and very submissive and grateful.   But they are very, very improvident.   So long as they have enough for to-day, let to-morrow look out for itself.   Even upon great festivals such as Christmas, when my husband would give them a double allowance of rations, they would come before our house, fire off their guns as a token of joy and thanks, and then proceed with their feast and never stop until they had the double allowance all eaten up and not a scrap left for the next day.

In my own sphere I was often quite amused with the young squaws.   They used to do my house-work for me. I would do each special thing for them—from cleaning, scrubbing, washing, cooking to sewing, fancy work, &c. and they would rival each other in learning to follow me. They would feel as proud when they could perform some simple little work, as a child feels when he has learned his A. B. Cs.   With time and care, good house-keepers could be made of many of them, and it is too bad to see so many clever, naturally gifted, bright creatures left in ignorance and misery. I think it was in Gray's Elegy that I read the line: "How many a flower is born to blush unseen, and waste its fragrance on the desert air."

When I look back over these three years, I feel a pang of more than sorrow. Ours was a happy home ; I grew to like my surroundings, I became fond of my Indian protegees, and to crown all, in December last, Mrs. Gowanlock came to live near us. I felt that even though a letter from home should be delayed, that I would not feel as lonesome as before. My husband was generous to a fault. He was liked by all the bands ;—our white neighbours were few, but they were splendid people, fast and true friends, and I might say since Mrs. Gowanlock arrived, I felt at home; I looked upon the place as my own, and the Indian children as my children; the same as my husband looked upon the men as his care, and they regarded him as a father. It was no longer to be a lonely life. It was to become a life of usefulness, joy, labor, peace and contentment. Such was the vision I had of the future, about the middle of last winter! But who knows what is in store for us! " There is a Providence that shapes our ends, rough-hew them as we will!"

I will here quote a few lines from deposition given at Regina: "When he, (my husband) first came up here, he had five bands to look after until a year ago, when the Chippewans were taken from his supervision and given to Mr. John Fitzpatrick. A little later, Mr. Fitzpatrick was transferred to another jurisdiction, and the Chippewans came again under my husband's care. He then had to look after the Chippewans, Oneepewhayaws, Mistoo-Kooceawsis and Puskeakeewins, and last year he had Big Bear's tribe. He was so engaged when the outbreak took place. All the Indians were very peacably inclined and most friendly to us all. My husband was much respected, and really beloved by all under his care, and they seemed to be most attached to him. We were, therefore, greatly astonished at their action towards us, but after all it was only Big Bear's followers that showed their enmity towards us. These too, pretended to be most friendly, and have often told us, "that but for my husband they would have starved."

With this, I close my second chapter, and will now, in the third offer my readers a picture of the scenes from the first of April last until the close of the struggle.

FROG LAKE SETTLEMENT—MR. DELANEY'S HOUSE ETC.

CHAPTER III.

THE NORTH-WEST TROUBLES.

THERE are scenes that are hard to properly describe. There are parts of our lives that can never be reproduced or transmitted to others upon paper.   As Father Abram J. Ryan, the Poet Priest of the South so beautifully tells us :

"But far on the deep there are billows,
  That never shall break on the beach ;
And I have heard Songs in the Silence,
  That never shall float into speech ;
And I have had dreams in the Valley,
  Too lofty for language to reach."

So with me and my story.   However I may have succeeded so far in expressing what I desired to convey to the public, I feel confident that I am far from able to do justice to to this last chapter.   The events crowd upon my mind in a sort of kaliedescope confusion and scarcely have the intention of giving expression to an idea, than a hundred others crop up to usurp its place in my mind.   Although I will tell the story of the tragic events as clearly and as truthfully as is possible, still I know that years after this little sketch is printed, I will remember incidents that now escape my memory.   One has not time, or inclination, when situated as I was, to take a cool survey of all that passes and commit to memory every word that might be said or remark that might be made.   Notwithstanding the fear I have of leaving out any points of interest or importance, I still imagine that my simple narrative will prove sufficient to give an idea, imperfect though it may be, of all the dangers we passed through, the sufferings we underwent, and the hair-breadth escapes we had.

Up to the 30th of March, 1885, we had not the fiaintest idea that a rebellion existed, nor that half-breeds and Indians were in open revolt.   On that day we received two letters, one from Captain Dickens, of Fort Pitt, and one from Mr. Rae, of Battleford.   Mr. Dickens' letter was asking all the whites to go down to Fort Pitt for safety as we could not trust the Indians ; and Mr. Rae's letter informed us of the "Duck Lake" battle and asking us to keep the Indians up there and not let them down to join Poundmaker.   When we were informed of the great trouble that was taking place, Mr. and Mrs. Gowanlock were apprised of the fact and they came up to our place for safety.   My husband had no fear for himself, but he had slight misgivings as to poor Mr. Quinn's situation.   Mr. Quinn was the agent in that district and was a Sioux half-breed. Johnny Pritchard, his interpreter, was a Cree half-breed.   My husband decided at once not to go to Fort Pitt. It would be a shame for us, he thought, to run away and leave all the Government provisions, horses, &c., at the mercy of those who would certainly take and squander them, moreover he feared nothing from the Indians.   His own band were perfectly friendly and good—and not ten days previous, Big Bear had given him a peace-pipe or *calumet*, and told him that he was beloved by all the band.

However, knowing the Indian character so well, and being aware that the more you seemed to confide in them the more you were liked by them, he and Mr. Quinn concluded to hold a council with the chiefs and inform them of the news from Duck Lake, impressing upon them the necessity of being good and of doing their work, and not minding those troublesome characters that were only bringing misery upon themselves.

Consequently, on the first of April, the council was held, but to their great astonishment and dismay, the Indians

knew more than they did about the affair, and, in fact, the
Indians knew all about the troubles, long before news ever
reached us, at Frog Lake, of the outbreak. At the council
were "Aimasis" (The King-bird), one of Big Bear's sons and
"The Wandering Spirit." They said that Big Bear had a
bad name, but now that he had a chance he would show
himself to be the whiteman's friend. All day, the 1st of
April, they talked and held council, and finally the Indians
went home, after shaking hands with my husband. They
then told him that the half-breeds intended to come our
way to join Riel ! that they also intended to steal our horses,
but that we need not fear as they (the Indians) would protect
us and make sure no horses would be taken and no harm
would be done. They also told us to sleep quiet and contented as they would be up all night and would watch. Big
Bear, himself, was away upon a hunt and only got to the
camp that night, we did not see him until next morning.
During that day, the Indians, without an exception, asked for
potatoes and of course they got them. They said we did
not need so much potatoes and they would be a treat for
them as they meant to make a big feast that night and have a
dance.

Now as to their statement about the half-breeds coming
to take horses or anything else we did not know whether to
believe them or not. Of course it would never do to pre-
tend to disbelieve them. However, the shadow of a doubt
hung over each of us. We knew that the Indians had a
better knowledge of all that was taking place than we had,
and since they knew so much about the troubles, it looked
probable enough that they should know what movements
the half-breeds were to make. And moreover, they seemed
so friendly, so good-spirited and in fact so free from any appearance of being in bad humor, that it would require a
very incredulous character not to put faith in their words

But on the other hand it seemed strange, that, if they knew so much about our danger, they never even hinted it to us until our men first spoke of it to them. However, be these things as they may, we felt secure and still something told us that all was not well : often to others as well as to Campbell's wizard,

> "The sun set of life, gives them mystical lore—
> And coming events cast their shadows before."

Thus we parted on the night of the first of April, and all retired to bed, to rest, to dream. Little did some amongst us that it was to be their last sleep, their last rest upon imagine earth, and that before another sun would set, they would be "sleeping the sleep that knows no waking"—resting the great eternal rest from which they will not be disturbed until the trumpet summons the countless millions from the tomb. Secure as we felt ourselves, we did not dream of the deep treachery and wicked guile that prompted those men to deceive their victims. The soldier may lie down calmly to sleep before the day of battle, but I doubt if we could have reposed in such tranquility if the vision of the morrow's tragedy had flashed across our dreams. It is indeed better that we know not the hour, nor the place ! And again, is it not well that we should ever be prepared, so that no matter how or when the angel of death may strike, we are ready to meet the inevitable and learn "the great Secret of Life and Death !"

At about half past-four on the morning of the second of April, before we were out of bed, Johnny Pritchard and Aimasis came to our house and informed my husband that the horses had been stolen by the half-breeds. This was the first moment that a real suspicion came upon our mind. Aimasis protested that he was so sorry. He said that no one, except himself and men, were to blame. He said that they danced nearly all night and when it got on towards morning that all fell asleep, and that the half-breeds must have been upon the watch, for it was then that they came and stole the horses. The two then left us and we got up· About an hour after, Aimises came back and told us not to mind the horses, as they would go and hunt for them and bring them back.

I since found out, that as the horses were only two miles away in the woods, they feared that my husband might go and find them himself and that their trick would be discovered. It is hard to say how far they intended, at that time, to go on with the bad work they had commenced.

In about half an hour some twenty Indians came to the house, Big Bear was not with them, nor had they on war-paint, and they asked for our guns, that is my husband's and Mr. Quinn's. They said they were short of firearms and that they wished to defend us against the half-breeds. No matter what our inclinations or misgivings might then be, we could not however refuse the arms. They seemed quite pleased and went away. An hour had scarcely elapsed when over thirty Indians painted in the most fantastic and hedious manner came in. Big Bear also came, but he wore no war-paint. He placed himself behind my husband's chair. We were all seated at the table taking our breakfast. The Indians told us to eat plenty as we would not be hurt. They also ate plenty themselves—some sitting, others standing, scattered here and there through the room, devouring as if they had fasted for a month.

Big Bear then remarked to my husband that there would likely be some shooting done, but for him not to fear, as the Indians considered him as one of themselves. Before we had our meal finished Big Bear went out. The others then asked us all to go up to the church with them. We consequently went, Mr. and Mrs. Gowanlock, Mr. Dill, Mr. Williscraft, my husband and myself.

When we arrived at the church the mass was nearly over. The Indians, on entering, made quite a noise and clatter. They would not remove their hats or head-dresses, they would not shut the door, nor remain silent, in fact, they did anything they considered provoking and ugly. The good priest, the ill-fated Father Fafard, turned upon the altar and addressed them. He warned them of the danger of excitement and he also forbade them to do any harm. He told them to go quietly away to their camps and not disturb the happinesss and peace of the community. They seemed to pay but little attention to what they heard, but continued the same tumult. Then Father Fafard took off his vestments and cut short the mass, the last that he was destined ever to say upon earth ; the next sacrifice he would offer was to be his own life. He as little dreamed as did some of the others that before many hours their souls would be with God, and that their bodies would find a few days sepulchre beneath that same church, whose burnt ruins would soon fall upon their union in the clay.

The Indians told us that we must all go back to our place. We obeyed and the priests came also. When we reached the house the Indians asked for beef-cattle. My husband gave them two oxen. Some of the tribe went out to kill the cattle. After about an hour's delay and talk, the Indians told us to come to their camp so that we would all be together and that they could aid us the better against the half-breeds. We consequently started with them.

Up to this point, I might say, the Indians showed us no ill-will, but continually harped upon the same chord, that they desired to defend and to save us from the half-breeds. So far they got everything they asked for, and even to the last of the cattle, my husband refused nothing. We felt no dread of death at their hands, yet we knew that they were excited and we could not say what they might do if provoked. We now believed that the story of the half-breeds was to deceive us and throw us off our guard—and yet we did not suspect that they meditated the foul deeds that darkened the morning of the second of April, and that have left it a day unfortunately, but too memorable, in the annals of Frog Lake history.

When I now look back over the events, I feel that we all took a proper course, yet the most unfortunate one for those that are gone. We could have no idea of the murderous intentions on the part of the Indians. Some people living in our civilized country may remark, that it was strange we did not notice the peculiar conduct of the Indians. But those people know nothing either of the Indian character or habits. So far from their manner seeming strange, or extraordinary, I might say, that I have seen them dozens of times act more foolishly, ask more silly questions and want more rediculous things—even appear more excited. Only for the war-paint and what Big Bear had told us, we would have had our fears completely lulled by the seemingly open and friendly manner. I have heard it remarked that it is a wonder we did not leave before the second of April and go to Fort Pitt ; I repeat, nothing at all appeared to us a sign of alarm, and even if we dreaded the tragic scenes, my husband would not have gone. His post was at home ; he had no fear that the Indians would hurt him ; he had always treated them well and they often acknowledged it ; he was an employee of the Government and had a trust in hand ; he would never have run away and left the Government horses, cattle, stores, provisions, goods, &c., to be divided and scattered amongst the bands, he even said so before the council day. Had he ran away and saved his life, by the act, I am certain he would be then blamed as a coward and one not trustworthy nor faithful to his position. I could not well pass over this part of our sad story without answering some of those comments made by people, who, neither through experience nor any other means could form an idea of the situation. It is easy for me to now sit down and write out, if I choose, what ought to have been done ; it is just as easy for people safe in their own homes, far from the scene, to talk, comment and tell how they would have acted and what they would have done. But these people know no more about the situation or the Indians, than I know about the Hindoos, their mode of life, or their habits.

Before proceeding any further with my narrative—and I am now about to approach the grand and awful scene of the tragedy—I will attempt, as best I can, to describe the Indian war-paint—the costume, the head-dress and attitudes. I imagined once that all the stories that American novelists told us about the war-dance,—war-whoops,—war-paint,—war-hatchet or tomahawk, were but fiction drawn from some too lively imaginations. But I have seen them in reality, more fearful than they have ever been described by the pen of novelist or pencil of painter.

Firstly, the Indians adorn their heads with feathers, about six inches in length and of every imaginable color. These they buy from the Hudson Bay Company. Also it is from the Company they procure their paints. An Indian, of certain bands, would prefer to go without food than be deprived of the paint. Our Indians never painted, and in fact Big Bear's band use to laugh at the Chippewans for their quiet manners and strict observance of their religious duties. In fact these latter were very good people and often their conduct would put to the blush white people. They never would eat or even drink a cup of tea without first saying a grace, and then, if only by a word, thanking God for what they received. But those that used the paint managed to arrange their persons in the most abomonable and ghastly manner. With the feathers, they mix porcupine quills and knitt the whole into their hair—then daub their head with a species of white clay that is to be found in their country. They wear no clothing except what they call loin-cloth or breach-cloth, and when they go on the war-path, just as when they went to attack Fort Pitt, they are completely naked. Their bodies are painted a bright yellow, over the forehead a deep green, then streaks of yellow and black, blue and purple upon the eyelids and nose. The streaks are a deep crimson, dotted with black, blue, or green. In a word, they have every imaginable color. It is hard to form an idea of how hedious they appear when the red, blue, green and white feathers deck the head, the body a deep orange or bright yellow and the features tatooed in all fantastic forms. No circus clown could ever equal their ghostly decorations. When one sees, for the first time, these horrid creatures, wild, savage, mad, whether in that war-dance or to go on the war-path, it is sufficient to make the blood run cold, to chill the senses, to unnerve the stoutest arm and strike terror into the bravest heart.

Such was their appearance, each with a "greenary-yellowy" hue, that one assumes when under the electric light, when we all started with them for their camp. We were followed and surrounded by the Indians. The two priests, Mr. and Mrs. Gowanlock, Mr. Gilchrist, Mr. Williscraft, Mr. Dill, Mr. Gouin, Mr. Quinn, my husband and myself formed the party of whites. My husband and I walked ahead. When we had got about one acre from the house we heard shots, which we thought were fired in the air. We paid little or no attention to them. I had my husband by the arm. We were thus linked when old Mr. Williscraft rushed past, bear-headed. I turned my head to see what was the cause of his excitement, when I saw Mr. Gowanlock fall. I was about to speak when I felt my husband's arm drop from mine— and he said, "I am shot too." Just then the priests rushed up and Father Fafard was saying something in French, which I could not catch. My husband staggered over about twenty feet from me and then back again and fell down beside me. I bent down and raised his head upon my lap. I think over forty shots must have been fired, but I could not tell what side the shot came from that hit my husband. I called Father Fafard and he came over. He knelt down and asked my husband if he could say the "confiteor." My husband said "yes" and then repeated the prayer from end to end. As he finished the prayer, the priest said : "my poor brother, I think you are safe with God," and as the words died upon his lips he received his death-wound and fell prostrate across my husband. I did not see who fired the shot. I only saw one shot fired ; I thought it was for myself but it was for my husband and it finished him. In a couple of minutes an Indian, from the opposite side, ran up, caught me by the wrist and told me to go with him. I refused, but I saw another Indian shake his head at me and tell me to go on. He dragged me, by force away. I got one glance—the last—at my poor husband's body and I was taken off. After we had gone a piece I tried to look back—but the Indian gave me a few shakes pretty roughly and then dragged me through the creek up to my waist in water— then over a path full of thorns and briars and finally flung me down in his tent.

I will not now stay to describe my feelings or attempt to give in language, an idea of the million phantoms of dread and terror ; memory seemed but too keen, and only too vividly could I behold the repetition of the scenes that had just passed before me. I stayed all day in the tent. I had the hope that some one would buy me off. Yet the hope was mingled with dispair. I thought if I could see Alec, one of our own Indians, that he would buy me, but I could not find out were he was. Towards evening I went to Johnny

Pritchard's tent and asked him to buy me.   He said he had been trying all day but could not succeed, however he expected to strike a bargain before night.   He had only one horse and the Indians wanted two horses for me.   As good luck would have it, he got Nolin—another half-breed—to give the second horse.   It was all they had and yet they willingly parted with that *all*, to save me from inhuman treatment, and even worse than a hundred deaths.   There was a slight relief in knowing that I was out of the power of the painted devil that held me, since my husband's death. But we were far from safe.   Pritchard took me to his own tent, and placed me with his wife and family.   There I felt that if there existed any chance of an escape at all I would be able to take advantage of it.   I fully trusted to Pritchard's manliness and good character, and I was not deceived.   He not only proved himself a sincere friend and a brave fellow, but he acted the part of a perfect gentleman, throughout, and stands, ever since, in my estimation the type of God's noblest creatures—A TRULY GOOD MAN.

For three weeks I was watched, as a cat would watch a mouse.   All night long the Indians kept prowling about the tent, coming in, going out, returning ; they resembled, at times, a pack of wolves skulking around their prey, and, at times, they appeared to resemble a herd of demons as we see them represented in the most extravagant of frightful pictures.   However, Pritchard spoke to them and their attentions became less annoying.   They may have watched as closely as ever and I think they did, but they seldom came into my tent and when they did come in, it was only for a moment.   I slept in a sitting position and whenever I would wake up, in a startled state from some fevered dream, I invariably saw, at the tent door, a human eye riveted upon me.

Imagine yourself seated in a quiet room at night, and

every time you look at the door, which is slightly ajar, you catch the eye of a man fixed upon you, and try then to form an idea of my feelings. I heard that the human eye had power to subdue the most savage beast that roams the woods; if so, there must be a great power in the organ of vision; but I know of no object so awe-inspiring to look upon, as the naked eye concentrated upon your features. Had we but the same conception of that "all seeing eye," which we are told, continually watches us, we would doubtlessly be wise and good; for if it inspired us with a proportionate fear, we would possess what Solomon tells us in the first step to wisdom—"The fear of the Lord is the beginning of wisdom."

But I never could describe all the miseries I suffered during those few weeks. I was two months in captivity; and eight days afterwards we heard of Major-General Strange's arrival, I managed to escape. The morning of our escape seemed to have been especially marked out by providence for us. It was the first and only time the Indians were not upon the close watch. Up to that day, we used to march from sunrise to sunset, and all night long the Indians would dance. I cannot conceive how human beings could march all day, as they did, and then dance the wild, frantic dances that they kept up all night. Coming on grey dawn they would tier out and take some repose. Every morning they would tear down our tent to see if we were in it. But whether attracted by the arrival of the soldiers—by the news of General Strange's engagement—or whether they considered we did not meditate flight, I cannot say—but most certainly they neglected their guard that day.

Some of them came in as usual, but we were making tea, and they went off. As soon as the coast was clear we left our tea, and all, and we departed. Maybe they did not know which way we went, or perhaps they were too much engaged with their own immediate danger to make chase, but be that as it may, we escaped. It was our last night under the lynx-eyed watchers. We went about two miles in the woods, and there hid. So far I had no covering for my head, and but scant raiment for my body. The season was very cold in April and May, and many a time I felt numb, chill, and sick, but there was no remedy for it ; only "grin and go through." In the last part of my captivity, I suffered from exposure to the sun. The squaws took all my hats, and I could not get anything to cover my head, except a blanket, and I would not dare to put one on, as I knew not the moment we might fall in with the scouts, and they might take me for a squaw. My shawl had become ribbons from tearing through the bush, and towards the end I was not able to get two rags of it to remain together. There is no possibility of giving an idea of our sufferings. The physical pains, exposures, dangers, colds, heats, sleepless nights, long marches, scant food, poor raiment, &c., would be bad enough,—but we must not loose sight of the mental anguish, that memory, only too faithful, would inflict upon us, and the terror that alternate hope and despair would compel us to undergo. I cannot say which was the worst. But when united, our sad lives seemed to have passed beneath the darkest cloud that could possibly hang over them.

When the Indians held their tea-dances or pow-wows in times of peace, the squaws and children joined in, and it was a very amusing sight to watch them. We often went three miles to look at a tea-dance, and I found it as attractive and interesting as a big circus would be to the children of a civilized place. But I had then no idea of the war-dance. They differ in every respect. No fire-arms are used at the tea-dance, and the guns and tomahawks and knives play the principal part in the war dance. A huge fire throws its yellow, fitful light upon the grim spectre-like objects that bound, leap, yell and howl, bend and pass, aim their weapons, and using their tomahawks in a mimic warfare, a hideous pantomine, around and across the blaze. Their gesticulations summon up visions of murder, horror, scalps, bleeding and dangling at their belts, human hearts and heads fixed upon their spears; their yells resemble at times the long and distant howl of a pack of famished wolves, when on the track of some hapless deer; and again their cries, their forms, their actions, their very surroundings could be compared to nothing else than some infernal scene, wherein the demons are frantic with hell, inflamed passions. Each one might bear Milton's description in his "Paradise Lost," of Death:

> "The other shape—
> If shape it might be called, that shape had none,
> Distinguishable, in member, joint or limb:
> *   *   *   *   *   *   *   *
> black it stood as night.
> Fierce as ten Furies, terrible as hell,
> And shook a dreadful dart.—"

And the union of all such beings might also be described in the words of the same author:

> "The chief were those who from the pit of hell,
> Roaming to seek their prey on earth, durst fix
> Their seats, long after, next the seat of God,
> Their altars, by his altar; gods adored
> Among the nations round; and durst abide
> Jehovah thundering out of Sion, throned
> Between the cherubim; yea of ten placed
> Within his sanctuary itself their shrines,
> Abominations; and with cursed things
> His holy rites and solemn feasts profaned."

The scenes at the little church the morning of the second of April,—the massacre of God's anointed priests, the desecration of the temple, the robbery of the sacred vessels and ornaments, the burning of the edifice—are not those the deeds of beings not human, but infernal? Is the likeness too vivid or too true? But in the wild banquet of their triumph, while still holding the sacred vessels, they were checked as of old was Belshazzer. Those scenes shall never pass from my memory ; with Freneau I can say:

> "And long shall timorous fancy see,
>   The painted chief, the pointed spear;
> And reason's self shall bow the knee,
>   To shadows and delusions here."

Now that I have passed once more over the trying scenes of the sad and eventful month of April, I will describe some of the dangers of our position, how we moved, camped, slept, and cooked. I will come to the transition from wild adventure to calm security, from the dangers of the wilderness to the safety of civilization. Once free from the toils of the Indians and back in the bosom of society, I will have but to describe our trip home, tell of the kindness received, and close this short sketch, bid "good-bye" to my kind and patient readers and return to that quiet life, which God in His mercy has reserved for me.

After our escape, we travelled all day long in the same bush, so that should the Indians discover us, we would seem to be still with them. We had nothing to eat but bread and water. We dare not make fire as we might be detected by the savages and then be subjected to a stricter *surveillance*, and maybe punished for our wanderings. Thus speaking of fire makes me think of the signals that the bands had, the beacons that flared from the heights at stated times and for certain purposes. Even before the outbreak, I remember of Indians coming to my husband and telling him that they were going on a hunt, and if such and such a thing took place, they would at a certain time and in a certain direction, make a fire. We often watched for the fires and at the stated time we would perceive the thin column of smoke ascend into the sky. For twenty and thirty miles around these fires can be seen. They are made in a very peculiar manner. The Indian digs a hole about a foot square and in that start the flame. He piles branches or fagots up in a cone fashion, like a bee-hive, and leaving a small hole in the top for the smoke to issue forth, he makes a draught space below on the four sides. If the wind is not strong, that tiny column of blue smoke will ascend to a height often of fifty or sixty feet. During the war times they make use of these fires as signals from band to band, and each fire has a conventional meaning. Like the *phares* that flashed the alarm from hill-top to hill-top or the tocsin that sang from belfry to belfry in the Basse Bretagne, in the days of the rising of the Vendee, so those beacons would communicate as swiftly the tidings that one band or tribe had to convey to another. Again, speaking of the danger of fire-making, I will give an example of what those Indians did with men of their own tribe.

A few of their men desired to go to Fort Pitt with their families, while the others objected. The couple of families escaped and reached the opposite side of a large lake. The Indians did not know which direction the fugitives had taken until noon the following day, when they saw their fire for dinner, across the lake. They started, half by one side and half by the other side of the lake, and came up so as to surround the fugitives. They took their horses, blankets, provisions, and camps, and set fire to the prairie on all sides so as to prevent the unhappy families from going or returning. When they thus treated their own people, what could white people expect at their hands?

The second day after our escape we travelled through a thicker bush and the men were kept busy cutting roads for us. We camped four times to make up for the day before, its fast and tramp. We made a cup of tea and a bannock each time. The third day we got into the open prairie, and about ten in the morning we lost our way. We were for over

three hours in perplexity. We feared to advance too much as we might be getting farther from our proper track. About one o'clock the sun appeared and by means of it we regained our right course. At four we camped for the night. We found a pretty clump of poplars and there pitched our tents for a good repose. I had just commenced to make a bannock for our tea, when Pritchard ran in and told me that the police were outside and for me to go to them at once. I sincerely believe that it was at that moment we ran the greatest of all our risks. The police had taken us for a band of Indians, and were on the point of shooting at us when I came out and arrested the act. When they found who we were, they came in, placed their guns aside, and gave us some corned beef and "hard tack," a species of biscuit. These were luxuries to us, while out tea and bannock were a treat to them. We all had tea together, and then we went with them to the open prairie, where we travelled for about two hours. Next morning we moved into Fort Pitt. It was a glad sight to see the three steamboats, and both sailors, soldiers, and civilians gave me a grand reception.

It was upon Friday morning that we got into Fort Pitt, and we remained their until Sunday. On Friday night the military band came down two miles to play for us. It was quite an agreeable change from the "tom-tom" of the Indians. Next day we went to see the soldiers drill. If I am not mistaken there were over 500 men there. Sunday, we left per boat, for Battleford, and got in that night. We had a pleasant trip on the steamer "The Marquis." While at Fort Pitt we had cabins on board the very elegant vessel "North West." We remained three weeks at Battleford, expecting to be daily called upon as witnesses in some cases. We travelled overland from Battleford to Swift Current, and thence by rail to Regina. At Moose Jaw, half way between Swift Current and Regina, we were greatly frightened. Such a number of people were collected to see and greet us, that we imagined it was Riel and his followers who had come to take us prisoners. Our fears were however, soon quelled. We remained four days at Regina; thence we came to Winnipeg. There we remained from Monday evening until Tuesday evening. Mostly all the people in the city came to see us, and I cannot commence to enumerate the valuable presents we received from the open-hearted citizens. We stoped with a Mrs. Bennett; her treatment to us, was like the care of a fond mother for her lost children.

We left on Thursday evening for Port Arthur, and thence we came by boat, to Owen Sound. A person not in trouble could not help but enjoy the glorious trip on the bosom of that immense inland sea. But, although we were overjoyed to be once more in safety, and drawing nearer our homes, yet memory was not sleeping, and we had too much to think off to permit our enjoying the trip as it could be enjoyed. From Owen Sound we proceeded to Parkdale by train. Parkdale is a lovely spot just outside of Toronto. I spent the afternoon there, and at nine o'clock that night left for home. I said good-bye to Mrs. Gowanlock; after all our sorrows, troubles, dangers, miseries, which we partook in union, we found it necessary to separate. And although we scarcely were half a year acquainted, it seemed as if we had been playmates in childhood, and companions throughout our whole lives. But, as we could not, for the present, continue our hand-in-hand journey, we separated merely physically speaking—for "time has not ages, nor space has not distance," to sever the recollections of our mutual trials.

I arrived home at 6 o'clock on Monday morning. What were my feelings as I stepped down from the hack, at that door, where three years before I stepped up into a carriage, accompanied by my husband! How different the scene of the bride leaving three years ago, and the widow returning to day!   Still, on the first occasion there were tears of regret at parting, and smiles of anticipated pleasure and happiness— on the second occasion there are tears of memory, and yet smiles of relief on my escape, and happiness in my safe return.

My story draws to a close "Like a tale that is told," it possesses, perhaps, no longer any interest for my readers. Yet, before dropping the veil upon the past, and returning to that life, out of which I had been forced by adverse circumstances.   Before saying good-bye to the public forever, I feel that I have a few concluding remarks which I should make, and which I will now offer to my readers as an *adieu!*

CONCLUSION.

ST. THOS. A. KEMPIS, in his beautiful " Imitation of Christ," asks: "who is it that has all which he wishes for? Not I, not you, nor any man upon earth." Although, we often are disappointed in our expectations of happiness, and fail to attain all we desire, yet we have much to be thankful for. I have passed through more than I ever expected I would be able to bear; and still I feel most grateful, and I would not close this short sketch, without addressing a few words to those who are objects of my gratitude.

Firstly, to my readers, I will say that all I have told you, in these few passages, is the simple truth; nothing added thereto, nothing taken therefrom. You have toiled through them despite the poverty of composition and the want of literary style upon them; and now that the story is told, I thank you for your patience with me, and I trust that you may have enjoyed a few moments of pleasure at least, while engaged in reading.

Secondly, let me say a word to my friends of the North-West, and to those of Canada, I cannot name anyone in particular, as those whose kindness was great, yet whose names were accidently omitted, would feel perhaps, that I slighted their favors. Believe me, one and all, that (in the words of a great orator of the last century), "my memory shall have mouldered when it ceases to recall your goodness and kindness, my tongue shall forever be silent, when it ceases to repeat your expressions of sympathy, and my heart shall have ceased to beat when it throbs no longer for your happiness."

The troubles of the North-West have proven that there is no land, however, happy, prosperous or tranquil it may be, that is totally free from the dangers of internal revolts,—it has likewise proven that our country possesses the means, the strength, the energy and stamina, to crush the hydra of disunion or rebellion, no matter where it may appear.   For like the upas tree, if it is permitted to take root and grow, its proportions would soon become alarming, while its poisonous influence would pollute the atmosphere with misery, ruin, rapine and death.

The rebellion is now a thing of the past.   It is now a page in Canadian history.   When a few generations shall come and go; our sad story of the "Frog Lake Massacre," may be totally forgotten, and the actors therein consigned to oblivion; but, these few papers, should they by any chance, survive the hand of time, will tell to the children of the future Canada, what those of your day experienced and suffered ; and when those who are yet to be, learn the extent of the troubles undergone, and the sacrifices made by those of the present, to set them examples worthy of imitation, and models fit for their practice, to build up for them a great and solid nation, they may perhaps reflect with pride upon the history of their country, its struggles, dangers, tempests and calms.   In those days, I trust and pray that Canada may be the realization of that glowing picture of a grand nation, drawn by a Canadian poet:—

> "The Northern arch, whose grand proportions,
>   Spans the sky from sea to sea,
> From Atlantic to Pacific—
>   Home of unborn millions free!"

The heartfelt sympathy of the country has been expressed in many forms, and ever with deep effect, and has twined a garland to drop upon the graves of those who sleep to-night away in the wilds of the North-West.   Permit me to add one flower to that chaplet.   You who are mothers, and know the value of your dutiful sons, while living, and have felt the greatness of their loss, when dead; you, who are sisters, and have known a brother's affection, the recollection of which draws you at times to his last resting place, to decorate that home of the dead with a forget-me-not; you, above all, who have experienced the love and devotion of a husband, and have mourned over that flower which has forever faded in death—you will not hesitate in joining with me, as I express, though feebly, my regret, and bring my sincerest of tributes to place upon the lonely grave by the Saskatchewan. Its united waters will sing their *requiem* while I say with Whittier:

> "Green be the turf above thee,
>   Friend of my better days;
> None knew thee but to love thee,
>   None named thee but to praise!"

END.

FATHER FAFARD.

REV. ADELARD FAFARD.

LEON ADELARD FAFARD, as the name denotes, was a French Canadian, born at St. Cuthbert, in the County of Berthier, Province of Quebec, on the 8th of June 1850. He was a son of Mr. Charles Fafard, cultivator, St. Cuthbert, and brother of Dr. Chas. Fafard, Jr., Amherst, Montreal. He entered the College of the Assumption on September 1st, 1864. From early years, he was devoted to his religion, and an enthusiastic student. He entered a monastic life on the 28th of June, 1872, and took his first vows on the 29th of June, 1873, one year later, and his perpetual vows on June the 29th, 1874.

In the Catholic Mission No. 839, July 3rd, 1885, Monseignor Grandire, says, Poor Father Fafard belonged to the Diocese of Montreal; he entered our congregation in 1872, and received his commission for my missions in 1875. I ordained him priest on December 8th, 1875, and sent him successively on missons to the savages under the direction of an experienced father. He was always distinguished for his zeal and good tact. For nearly two years he was Superior of a district, and by superhuman efforts succeeded in making a fine establishment by working himself, as a hired laborer, in order to diminish the expenses of his district.

Rev. P. Lebert speaks of him as a pious, humble, subdued, very obedient, full of good will and courage. He adds that he had talent and showed a good disposition for preaching ; his voice was full and strong, and his health robust. He was beginning to see the fruits of his labors, when on the 2nd of April, 1885, he was so fouly murdered while administering consolation to dying men.

MR. DILL.

MR. DILL.

EO. DILL who was massacred at Frog Lake, was born in the Village of Preston, in the County of Waterloo, Ont., and was at the time of his death about 38 years of age. At the age of about 17 years, he joined his brother, who was then trading for furs at Lake Nipissing, in 1864. In 1867 his brother left Nipissing, leaving him the business, which he continued for a few years, when he left that place and located on a farm on Bauchere Lake in the Upper Ottawa River. In 1872 he went to Bracebridge, Muskoka, where his brother, Mr. J. W. Dill, the present member for the Local Legislature, had taken up his residence and was doing business. After a short time, he set up business as a general store at Huntsville, where he remained until 1880; he then took a situation in a hardware store in the Village of Bracebridge. While living in Huntsville, he was married to Miss Cassleman, of that place. They had a family of two children, who are now living somewhere in Eastern Canada. In 1882, at the time of the Manitoba boom, he went to see that country, and engaged with a Dominion Land Surveyor, retiring to Bracebridge again in the winter following, remaining till spring 1883, he again went to the North-West, and again engaged with a Surveyor; his object was to secure a good location and settle down to farming, but his inclination led him to trading again, and after speculating until the fall of 1884, he left Battleford for Frog Lake.

He was the only trader in the Frog Lake district, and was well respected by the community generally.

THE SASKATCHEWAN STREAM.

MR. DELANEY while in Ontario on a visit from the North-West, in the year 1882, for the purpose of taking back a bride, gave vent to the following beautiful words:

I long to return to the far distant West,
Where the sun on the prairies sinks cloudless to rest,
Where the fair moon is brightest and stars twinkling peep;
And the flowers of the wood soft folded in sleep.

Oh, the West with its glories, I ne'er can forget,
The fair lands I found there, the friends I there met,
And memory brings back like a fond cherished dream;
The days I have spent by Saskatchewan stream.

By dark Battle river, in fancy I stray,
And gaze o'er the blue Eagle Hills far away,
And hark to the bugle notes borne o'er the plain,
The echoing hills giving back the refrain.

Ah, once more I'll go to my beautiful West,
Where nature is loveliest, fairest and best:
And lonely and long do the days to me seem,
Since I wandered away from Saskatchewan stream.

Ontario, home of my boyhood farewell,
I leave thy dear land in a fairer to dwell,
Though fondly I love thee, I only can rest,
'Mid the flower strewn prairie I found in the West

And as by the wide rolling river I stray,
Till death comes at night like the close of the day,
The moon from the bright starry heavens shall gleam
On my home by the banks of Saskatchewan stream.

CONTENTS.

PART I.

ILLUSTRATIONS.

Over 15,000 in use.

FAULTLESS

SQUARE, SPLENDID.

High Art and Low Feed Base Burner, with Round Sectional
Fire Pot.

The Toronto Stove & Mf'g Co., 'Ltd.'

PARKDALE, TORONTO,

Manufacturers of the Celebrated **DIAMOND A RANGE**
Coal and Wood Cooks, Box and Round Heaters.

LATEST AMERICAN DESIGNS.

SPECIAL CHEAP TRIPS

TO

FLORIDA, GEORGIA, TEXAS,

and all Southern points, will be run during the winter from Toronto and other stations of the

CANADIAN PACIFIC RAILWAY.

For rates, pamphlets and full particulars, send stamp to

THOMAS EDWARDS,

Office of Florida Excursions,

20 QUEEN ST., PARKDALE ONTARIO.

-:The Parkdale Times:-

PRINTING AND

PUBLISHING OFFICE.

We have erected a building suitable for carrying on the Printing Business in all its branches, and are prepared to take orders for all kinds of work.

We are confident that we can give satisfaction, our motto being punctuality, well executed and reasonable prices.

THE TIMES

Is Published every Friday, an excellent News Paper devoted to the family and a first-class advertising medium.

Subscription   -   -   per year 50 cents.

NO. 24 QUEEN STREET,
PARKDALE.

A. G. GOWANLOCK, Mgr.   JAS. GOWANLOCK, Agt.

Cynthia Ann Parker

The Story of Her Capture

James T. DeShields

Garland Publishing Inc., New York & London
1976

Copyright © 1976
by Garland Publishing, Inc.
All Rights Reserved

———

Bibliographical note:

this facsimile has been made from a copy in the
Newberry Library
(Ayer.256.P23.D4.1886)

———

Library of Congress Cataloging in Publication Data

De Shields, James T
   Cynthia Ann Parker : the story of her capture.

   (The Garland library of narratives of North American
Indian captivities ; v. 95)
   Reprint of the 1886 ed. printed for the author,
St. Louis.
   Issued with the reprint of the 1885 ed. of Gowanlock,
Theresa. Two months in the camp of Big Bear. New York,
1976.
   1. Parker, Cynthia Ann, 1827?-1864. 2. Comanche
Indians--Captivities. 3. Indians of North America--
Captivities. 4. Parker, Quanah, 1854-1911. 5. Ross,
Lawrence Sullivan, 1838-1898. I. Title. II. Series.

E85.G2 vol. 95 [E99.C85] 973'.04'97s [970'.004'97] [B]
ISBN 0-8240-1719-6   75-7121

Printed in the United States of America

CYNTHIA ANN PARKER.

CYNTHIA ANN PARKER.

THE STORY OF HER CAPTURE

At the Massacre of the Inmates of Parker's Fort; of her Quarter of a Century Spent Among the Comanches, as the Wife of the War Chief, Peta Nocona; and of her Recapture at the Battle of Pease River, by Captain L. S. Ross, of the Texian Rangers.

— BY —

JAMES T. DeSHIELDS,

Author of "Frontier Sketches," Etc.

"Truth is Stranger than Fiction."

ILLUSTRATED.

ST. LOUIS:
Printed for the Author.
1886,

Copyright 1886 by
JAMES T. DeSHIELDS.
All Rights Reserved.

CHAS. B. WOODWARD
Printing and Book Manufacturing Co.,
ST. LOUIS.

DEDICATED

(By Permission)

— TO —

GENL. L. S. ROSS,

— OF —

WACO, TEXAS.

PREFACE.

In the month of June, 1884, there appeared in the columns of the Forth Worth *Gazette* an advertisement signed by the Comanche chief, Quanah Parker, and dated from the reservation near Fort Sill, in the Indian Territory, enquiring for a photograph of his late mother, Cynthia Ann Parker, which served to revive interest in a tragedy which has always been enveloped in a greater degree of mournful romance and pathos than any of the soul-stirring episodes of our pioneer life, so fruitful of incidents of an adventurous nature.

From the valued narratives kindly furnished us by Victor M. Ross, Major John Henry Brown and Gen. L. S. Ross, supplemented by the Jas. W. Parker book and copious notes from Hon. Ben. F. Parker, together with most of the numerous partial accounts of the fall of Parker's Fort and subsequent relative events, published during the past fifty years; and after a careful investigation and study of the whole, we have laboriously and with much pains-taking, sifted out and evolved the foregoing narrative of plain, unvarnished facts, which form a part of the romantic history of Texas.

In the preparation of our little volume the thanks of the youthful author are due to Gen. L. S. Ross, of

Waco; Major John Henry Brown of Dallas; Gen. Walter P. Lane of Marshall; Col. John S. Ford of San Antonio; Rev. Homer S. Thrall—the eminent historian of Texas; Mr. A. F. Corning of Waco; Capt. Lee Hall, Indian Agent, I. T., and Mrs. C. A. Westbrook of Lorena, for valuable assistance rendered.

To Victor M. Ross of Laredo, Texas, the author has been placed under many and lasting obligations for valuable data so generously placed at his disposal, and that too at considerable sacrifice to the donor.

From this source we have obtained much of the matter for our narrative.

In submitting our little work—the first efforts of the youthful author—we assure the reader that while there are, doubtless, many defects and imperfections, he is not reading fiction, but facts which form only a part of the tragic and romantic history of the Lone Star State.

JAMES T. DeSHIELDS,

BELTON, Texas, May 19, 1886.

CONTENTS.

———

CYNTHIA ANN PARKER.

CHAPTER I.

The Parker Fort Massacre, Etc.

CONTEMPORARY with, and among the earliest of the daring and hardy pioneers that penetrated the eastern portion of the Mexican province of Texas, were the "Parker family," who immigrated from Cole county, Illinois, in the fall of the year 1833, settling on the west side of the Navasota creek, near the site of the present town of Groesbeck, in Limestone county, one or two of the family coming a little earlier and some a little later.

The elder John Parker was a native of Virginia, resided for a time in Elbert county, Georgia, but chiefly reared his family in Bedford county, Tennessee, whence in 1818 he removed to Illinois.

The family, with perhaps one or two exceptions, belonged to one branch of the primitive Baptist church, commonly designated as "two seed," or "hard shell" Baptists.

In the spring of 1834 the colonist erected Parker's Fort, [1]) a kind of wooden barricade, or wall around their cabins, which served as a means of better protecting themselves against the numerous predatory bands of Indians into that, then, sparsely settled section.

As early as 1829 the "Prairie Indians" had declared war against the settlers, and were now actively hostile,

---

1) The reader will understand by this term, not only a place of defense, but the residence of a small number of families belonging to the same neighborhood. As the Indian mode of warfare was an indiscriminate slaughter of all ages, and both sexes, it was as requisite to provide for the safety of the women and children as for that of the men.

Dodridge's faithful pen picture of early pioneer forts, will perhaps give the reader a glimps of old Fort Parker in the dark and bloody period of its existence. He says: .

"The *fort* consisted of cabins, blockhouses, and stockades. A range of cabins commonly formed on one side at least of the fort. Divisions, or portions of logs, separated the cabins from each other. The walls on the outside were ten or twelve feet high, the slope of the roof being turned wholly inward. A very few of these cabins had puncheon floors, the greater part were earthen. The blockhouses were built at the angles of the fort. They projected about two feet beyond the outer walls of the cabins and stockades. Their upper stories were about eighteen inches every way larger in dimension than the under one, leaving an opening at the commencement of the second to prevent the enemy from making a lodgment under their walls. In some forts, instead of blockhouses the angles of the fort were furnished with bastions. A large folding gate, made of thick slabs, nearest the spring, closed the fort. The stockades, bastions, cabins, and blockhouse walls, were furnished with port-holes at proper heights and distances. The whole of the outside was completely bullet-proof.

It may be truly said that "necessity is the mother of invention"; for the whole of this work was made without the aid of a single nail or spike of iron; and for this reason such things were not to be had. In some places, less exposed, a single blockhouse, with a cabin or two, constituted the whole fort. Such places of refuge may appear very trifling to those who have been in the habit of seeing the formidable military garrisons of Europe and America, but they answered the purpose, as the Indians had no artillery. They seldom attacked, and scarcely ever took one of them."

constantly committing depredations in different localities.

Parker's colony at this time consisted of only some eight or nine families, viz: Elder John Parker, patriarch of the family, and his wife; his son James W. Parker, wife, four single children and his daughter, Mrs. Rachel Plummer, her husband, L. M. T. Plummer, and infant son, fifteen months old; Mrs. Sarah Nixon, another daughter, and her husband L. D. Nixon; Silas M. Parker (another son of Elder John), his wife and four children; Benjamin F. Parker, an unmarried son of the Elder [2]); Mrs. Nixon, sr., mother of Mrs. James W. Parker; Mrs. Elizabeth Kellogg, daughter of Mrs. Nixon; Mrs. —— Duty; Samuel M. Frost, wife and two children; G. E. Dwight, wife and two children; in all thirty-four persons.

Besides those above mentioned, old man—— Lunn, David Faulkenberry and his son Evan, Silas Bates, and Abram Anglin, a boy, had erected cabins a mile or two distant from the fort, where they resided.

[2] Elder Daniel Parker, a man of strong mental powers, a son of Elder John, does not figure in these events. He signed the Declaration of Independence in 1836, and preached to his people till his death in Anderson county in 1845. Ex-Representative Ben. F. Parker, is his son and successor in preaching at the same place. Isaac Parker, above mentioned, another son, long represented Houston and Anderson counties in Senate and House, and in 1855 represented Tarrant county. He died in Parker county, not long since, not far from 88 years of age. Isaac D. Parker of Tarrant is his son.

These families were truly the advance guard of civilization of that part of our frontier. Fort Houston, in Anderson county, being the nearest protection, except their own trusty rifles.

Here the struggling colonist remained, engaged in the avocations of a rural life, tilling the soil, hunting buffalo, bear, deer, turkeys and smaller game, which served abundantly to supply their larder at all times with fresh meat, in the enjoyment of a life of Arcadian simplicity, virtue and contentment, until the latter part of the year 1835, when the Indians and Mexicans forced the little band of compatriots to abandon their homes, and flee with many others before the invading army from Mexico.

On arriving at the Trinity river they were compelled to halt in consequence of an overflow. Before they could cross the swollen stream the sudden and unexpected news reached them that Santa Anna and his vandal hordes had been confronted and defeated at San Jacinto, that sanguinary engagement which gave birth to the new sovereignty of Texas, and that TEXAS WAS FREE FROM MEXICAN TYRANNY.

On receipt of this news the fleeing settlers were overjoyed, and at once returned to their abandoned homes.

The Parker colony now retraced their steps, first going to Fort Houston, where they remained a few days in order to procure supplies, after which they made their way back to Fort Parker to look after their stock and to prepare for a crop.

These hardy sons of toil spent their nights in the fort, repairing to their farms early each morning.

On the night of May 18, 1836, all slept at the fort, James W. Parker, Nixon and Plummer repairing to their field a mile distant on the Navasota, early next morning, little thinking of the great calamity that was soon to befall them.

About 9 o'clock a. m. the fort was visited by several hundred[3]) Comanche and Kiowa Indians. On approaching to within about three hundred yards of the fort the Indians halted in the prairie, presenting a white flag; at the same time making signs of friendship.

At this time there were only six men in the fort, three having gone out to work in the field as above stated. Of the six men remaining, only five were able to bear arms, viz: Elder John Parker, Benjamin and Silas Parker, Samuel and Robert Frost. There were ten women and fifteen children.

The Indians, artfully feigning the treacherous semblance of friendship, pretented that they were looking for a suitable camping place, and enquired as to the exact

3) Different accounts have variously estimated the number of Indians at from 300 to 700. One account says 300, another 500, and still another 700. There were perhaps about 500 warriors.

locality of a water-hole in the vicinity, at the same time asking for a beef to appease their hungry—a want always felt by an Indian, when the promise of fresh meat loomed up in the distant perspective; and he would make such pleas with all the servile sicophancy of a slave, like the Italian who embraces his victim ere plunging the poniard into his heart.

Not daring to resent so formidable a body of savages, or refuse to comply with their requests, Mr. Benjamin F. Parker went out to them, had a talk and returned, expressing the opinion that the Indians were hostile and intented to fight, but added that he would go back and try to avert it. His brother Silas remonstrated, but he persisted in going, and was immediately sur- rounded and killed, whereupon the whole force—their savage instincts aroused by the sight of blood—charged upon the works, uttering the most terrific and unearth- ly yells that ever greeted the ears of mortals. Cries and confusion reigned. The sickening and bloody tragedy was soon enacted. Brave Silas M. Parker fell on the outside of the fort, while he was gallantly fight- ing to save Mrs. Plummer. Mrs. Plummer made a most manful resistance, but was soon overpowered, knocked down with a hoe and made captive. Samuel M. Frost and his son Robert met their fate while hero- ically defending the women and children inside the stockade. Old Granny Parker was outraged, stabbed and left for dead. Elder John Parker, wife and Mrs. Kellogg attempted to make their escape, and in the effort had gone about three-fourths of a mile, when they were overtaken and driven back near to the fort where the old gentleman was stripped, murdered, scalped and horribly mutilated. Mrs. Parker was stripped, speared and left for dead, but by feigning death escaped, as will be seen further on. Mrs. Kellogg was spared as a captive.

The result summed up, was as follows:

Killed—Elder John Parker, aged seventy-nine; Silas M. and Benjamin F. Parker; Samuel M. and his son Robert Frost.

Wounded dangerously—Mrs. John Parker; Old Granny Parker and Mrs.——Duty.

Captured—Mrs. Rachel Plummer, (daughter of James W. Parker), and her son James Pratt Plummer, two years of age; Mrs. Elizabeth Kellogg; Cynthia Ann Parker, nine years old, and her little brother John Parker, aged six years, children of Silas M. Parker. The remainder of the inmates making their escape, as we shall narrate.

When the attack on the fort first commenced, Mrs. Sarah Nixon made her escape and hastened to the field to advise her father, husband and Plummer. On her arrival, Plummer hurried on horseback to inform the Faulkenberrys, Lunn, Bates and Anglin. Parker and Nixon started to the fort, but the former met his family on the way, and carried them some five miles down the Navasota, secreting them in the bottom. Nixon, though unarmed, continued on towards the fort, and met Mrs. Lucy, wife of the dead Silas Parker, with her four children, just as they were intercepted by a small party of mounted and foot Indians. They compelled the mother to lift behind two mounted warriors her daughter Cynthia Ann, and her little son John. The foot Indians now took Mrs. Parker, her two youngest children and Nixon back to the fort.

Just as the Indians were about to kill Nixon, David Faulkenberry appeared with his rifle, and caused them to fall back. Nixon, after his narrow escape from death, seemed very much excited, and immediately left in search of his wife, soon falling in with Dwight, with his own and Frost's family. Dwight and party soon overtook J. W. Parker and went with him to the hiding place in the bottom.

Faulkenberry, thus left with Mrs. Parker and her two children, bade her to follow him. With the infant in her arms and leading the other child she obeyed. Seeing them leave the fort, the Indians made several feints, but were held in check by the brave man's rifle. Several mounted warriors, armed with bows and arrows strung and drawn, and with terrific yells would charge them, but as Faulkenberry would present his gun they would halt, throw up their shields, right about, wheel and retire to a safe distance. This continued for some distance, until they had passed through a prairie of some forty or fifty acres. Just as they were entering the woods, the Indians made a desperate charge, when one warrior, more daring than the others, dashed up so near that Mrs. Parker's faithful dog seized his horse by the nose, whereupon both horse and rider somersaulted, alighting on their backs in a ravine. Just at this moment Silas Bates, Abram Anglin and Evan Faulkenberry, armed, and Plummer unarmed, came up, causing the Indians to retire, after which the party made their way unmolested.

As they were passing through the field where the three men had been at work in the morning, Plummer, as if aroused from a dream, demanded to know what had become of his wife and child. Armed only with a butcher knife, he left the party, in search of his loved ones, and was seen no more for six days.

The Faulkenberrys, Lunn, with Mrs. Parker and children, secreted themselves in a small creek bottom, some distance from the first party, each unconcious of the other's whereabouts.

At twilight Abraham Anglin and Evan Faulkenberry started back to the fort to succor the wounded
and those who might have escaped. On their way,
and just as they were passing Faulkenberry's cabin,
Anglin saw his first and only ghost. He says, "It
was dressed in white with long, white hair streaming
down its back. I admit that I was worse scared at
this moment than when the Indians were yelling and
charging us. Seeing me hesitate, my ghost now
beckoned me to come on. Approaching the object it
proved to be old Granny Parker, whom the Indians
had wounded and stripped, with the exception of her
underwear. She had made her way to the house
from the fort by crawling the entire distance. I took
some bed clothing, and carrying her some distance
from the house, made her a bed, covered her up and
left her until we should return from the fort. On arriving at the fort we could not see a single individual
alive or hear a human sound. But the dogs were
barking, the cattle lowing, the horses neighing and
the hogs squealing, making a hideous and strange
meadly of sounds. Mrs. Parker had told me where
she had left some silver, $106.50. This I found
under a hickory bush by moonlight. Finding no one
at the fort we returned to where I had hid Granny
Parker. On taking her up behind me, we made our

way back to our hiding place in the bottom, where we found Nixon, whom we had not seen since his cowardly flight at the time he was rescued by Faulkenberry from the Indians." [4])

On the next morning, Bates, Anglin and E. Faulkenberry went back to the fort to get provisions and horses and to look after the dead. On reaching the fort they found five or six horses, a few saddles and some meal, bacon and honey. Fearing an attack from the red devils who might still be lurking around, they left without burying the dead. Returning to their comrades in the bottom, they all concealed themselves until the next night, when they started through the woods to Fort Houston, which place they reached without material suffering.

Fort Houston, an asylum on this as on many other occasions, stood on what has been for many years the farm of a wise statesman, a chivalrous soldier and a true patriot—John H. Reagan—two miles west of Palestine.

After wandering around and traveling for six days and nights, during which time they suffered much

(4—In the book published by James W. Parker on pages ten and eleven, he states that Nixon liberated Mrs. Parker from the Indians and rescued old Granny Parker. Mr. Anglin, in his account contradicts, or rather corrects this statement. He says: "I positively assert that this is a mistake and I am willing to be qualified to the statement I here make and can prove the same by Silas H. Bates, now living near Graesbeck."

from hunger and thirst, with their clothing torn into shreads, their bodies lacerated with briars and thorns, the women and children with unshod and bleeding feet, the party of James W. Parker ——————— men, and ————————[5]) women and children—reached Tinnin's, at the old San Antonio and Nacogdoches crossing of the Navasota. Being informed of their approach, Messrs. Carter and Courtney, with five horses, met them some miles away, and thus enabled the women and children to ride. The few people around, though but returned to their deserted homes after the victory of San Jacinto, shared all they had of food and clothing with them.

Plummer, after six days of wanderings alone in the wilderness, arrived at the fort the same day.

In due time the members of the party located temporarily as best suited the respective families, most of them returning to Fort Parker soon afterwards.

A burrial party of twelve men from Fort Houston went up and burried the dead. Their remains now repose near the site of old Fort Parker. Peace to their memories. Unadorned are their graves; not even a slab of marble or a memento of any kind has been erected to tell the traveler where rests the remains of this brave little band of pioneer heroes who wrestled with the savage for the mastery of this proud domain.

---

5) We are unable to ascertain the exact number. Different accounts variously estimate the number from 10 to 20.

After the massacre the savages retired with their booty to their own wild haunts amid the hills and valleys of the beautiful Canadian and Pease rivers.

CHAPTER II.

The Captives—Cynthia Ann and John Parker.

Of the captives we will briefly trace their subsequent checkered career.

After leaving the fort the two tribes, the Comanches and Kiowas, remained and traveled together until midnight. They then halted on an open prairie, staked out their horses, placed their pickets, and pitched their camp. Bringing all their prisoners together for the first time, they tied their hands behind them with raw-hide thongs so tightly as to cut the flesh, tied their feet close together, and threw them upon their faces. Then the braves, gathering around with their yet bloody, dripping scalps, commenced their usual war dance. They danced, screamed, yelled, stamping upon their prisoners, beating them with bows until their own blood came near strangling them. The remainder of the night these frail women suffered and had to listen to the cries and groans of their tender little children.

Mrs. Elizabeth Kellogg soon fell into the hands of the Keechis, from whom, six months after her capture, she was purchased by a party of Delawares, who carried her into Narogdoches and delivered her to

Gen: Houston, who paid them $150.00, the amount
they had paid and all they asked.

On the way thence to Fort Houston, escorted by
James W. Parker and others, a hostile Indian was
slightly wounded and temporarily disabled by a Mr.
Smith. Mrs. Kellogg instantly recognized him as the
savage who had scalped the patriarch, Elder John
Parker, whereupon, without judge, jury or court-mar-
tial, or even dallying with "Judge Lynch," he was
involentarily hastened to the "happy hunting grounds"
of his fathers.

Mrs. Rachel Plummer remained a captive about
eighteen months. Soon after her capture she was delivered of a child. The crying of her infant annoyed
her captors, and the mother was forced to yield up her
offspring to the merciless fiends,—in whose veins the
milk of human sympathy had never flowed,—to be
murdered before her eyes with all the demoniacal
demonstrations of brutality intact in those savages. The innocent little babe but six weeks old was
torn madly from the mother's bosom by six giant
Indians, one of them clutched the little prattling innocent by the throat, and like a hungry beast with defenseless prey, he held it out in his iron grasp until all
evidence of life seemed extinct. Mrs. Plummer's feeble efforts to save her child were utterly fruitless. They
tossed it high in the air and repeatedly let it fall on

rocks and frozen earth.   Supposing the child dead
they returned it to its mother, but discovering traces of
lingering life, they again, by force, tore it angrily from
her, tied plaited ropes around its neck and threw its
unprotected body into hedges of prickley pear.   They
would repeatedly pull it through these lacerating rushes
with demonic yells.   Finally, they tied the rope attached to its neck to the pommel of a saddle and rode
triumphantly around a circuit until it was not only dead
but litterly torn to shreds.   All that remained of that
once beautiful babe was then tossed into the lap of its
poor, distracted mother.   With an old knife the weeping mother was allowed to dig a grave and bury her
babe.

After this she was given as a servant to a very cruel
old squaw, who treated her in a most bruatl manner.
Her son had been carried off by another party to the
far West and she supposed her husband and father had
been killed at the massacre.   Her infant was dead, and
death to her would have been a sweet relief.   Life was
a burden, and driven almost to desperation, she re-
solved no longer to submit to the intolerant old squaw.
One day when the two were some distance from, although still in sight of the camp, her mistress attempted to beat her with a club.   Determined not to submit
to this, she wrenched the club from the hands of the
squaw and knocked her down.   The Indians, who had

witnessed the whole proceedings from their camp, now came running up, shouting at the top of their voices. She fully expected to be killed, but they patted her on the shoulder, crying, '' Bueno! bueno!!'' (Good! good!!) or well done! She now fared much better and soon became a great favorite and was known as the '' Fighting Squaw.'' She was eventually ransomed through the agency of some Mexican Santa Fe traders, by a noble-hearted, American merchant of that place, Mr. William Donahue. She was purchased in the Rocky Mountains so far north of Santa Fe that seventeen days were consumed in reaching that place. She was at once made a member of her benefactor's family, where she received the kindest of care and attention. Ere long she accompanied Mr. and Mrs. Donahue on a visit to Independence, Missouri, where she had the pleasure of meeting and embracing her brother-in-law, L. D. Nixon, and by him was escorted back to her people in Texas.[1]

On the 19th of February, 1838, she reached her father's house, exactly twenty-one months from her

(1—During her stay with the Indians, Mrs. Plummer had many thrilling adventures, which she often related after her reclamation. In narrating her reminiscences, she said that in one of her rambles, after she had been with the Indians some time, she discovered a cave in the mountains, and in company with the old squaw that guarded her, she explored it and found a large diamond, but her mistress immediately demanded it, and she was forced to give it up. She said also here in these mountains she saw a bush which had thorns on it resembling fish-hooks which the Indians used to catch fish with, and she herself has often caught trout with them in the little mountain streams.

capture.   She had never seen her little son, James Pratt,
since soon after their capture, and knew nothing of his
fate.   She wrote, or dictated a thrilling and graphic
history of her capture and the horrors of her captivity,
the tortures and hardships she endured, and all the incidents of her life with her captors, with observations
among the savages.[2]   In this book she tells the last she
saw of Cynthia Ann and John Parker.   She died on
the 19th of February, 1839, just one year after reaching home.   As a remarkable coincidence it may be
stated that she was born on the 19th, married on the
19th, captured on the 19th, released on the 19th,
reached Independence on the 19th, arrived at home on
the 19th, and died on the 19th of the month.

Her son, James Pratt Plummer, after six long and
weary years of captivity and suffering, during which
time he had lived among many different tribes and
traveled several thousand miles, was ransomed and
taken to Fort Gibson late in 1842, and reached home
in February, 1843, in charge of his grand-father.   He

(2—This valuable and interesting little book is now *rare, scarce* and
out of *print*.   The full title of the volume is:
"Narration of the Perilous Adventures, miraculous escapes and sufferings of Rev. Jas. W. Parker, during a frontier residence in Texas of
fifteen years.   With an impartial geographical description of the climate,
soil, timber, water, etc., of Texas."—To which is appended the narrative of the capture and subsequent sufferings of Mrs. Rachel Plummer
(his daughter) during a captivity of twenty-one months among the
Comanche Indians, etc.   18 mo, p. p. 95—35, boards.   Louisville, 1844.

became a respected citizen of Anderson county. Both he and his father are now dead.

This still left in captivity Cynthia and John Parker, who, as subsequently learned, were held by separate bands. The brother and sister thus separated, gradually forgot the language, manners and customs of their own people, and became thorough Comanches as the long years stole slowly away. How long the camera of their young brains retained impressions of the old home within the fort, and the loved faces of their pale-faced kindred, no one knows; though it would appear that the fearful massacre should have stamped an impress indellible while life continued. But the young mind, as the twig, is inclined by present circumstances, and often forced in a way wholly foreign to its native and original bent.

John grew up with the little semi-nude Comanche boys of his own age, and played at "hunter" and "warrior" with pop-guns made of the elder stem, or bows and arrows, and often flushed the chaparral for hare and grouse, or entrapped the finny denizens of the mountain brooks with the many peculiar and ingenious devices of the wild man for securing for his repast the toothsome trout which abounds so plentifully in that elevated and delightful region, so long inhabited by the lordly Comanches.

When just arrived at manhood, John accompanied a raiding party down the Rio Grande and into Mexico. Among the captives taken was a young Mexican girl of great beauty, to whom the young warrior felt his heart go out. The affection was reciprocated on the part of the fair Dona Juanita, and the two were soon engaged to be married, so soon as they should arrive at the Comanche village. Each day as the cavalcade moved leisurely, but steadily along, the lovers could be seen riding together, and discussing the anticipated pleasures of connubial life, when suddenly John was prostrated by a violent attack of small-pox. The cavalcade could not tarry, and so it was decided that the poor fellow should be left all alone in the vast *Llano Esticado* to die or recover as fate decreed. But the little Aztec beauty refused to leave her lover, insisting on her captors allowing her to remain and take care of him. To this the Indians reluctantly consented. With Juanita to nurse and cheer him up, John lingered, lived, and ultimately recovered, when, with as little ceremony, perhaps, as consummated the nuptials of the first pair in Eden, they assumed the matrimonial relation ; and Dona Juanita's predilections for the customs and comforts of civilization were sufficiently strong to induce her lord to abandon the wild and nomadic life of a savage for the comforts to be found in a straw-thatched *Jackal*. "They settled," says Mr.

Thrall, the historian of Texas, "on a stock ranch in the far West." When the civil war broke out John Parker joined a Mexican company in the Confederate service, and was noted for his gallantry and daring. He, however, refused to leave the soil of Texas, and would, under no circumstances, cross the Sabine into Louisiana. He was still living on his ranch across the Rio Grande a few years ago, but up to that time had never visited any of his relatives in Texas.

Of Cynthia Ann Parker (we will anticipate the thread of the narrative). Four long years have elapsed since she was cruelly torn from a mother's embrace and carried into captivity. During this time no tidings have been recieved of her. Many efforts have been made to ascertain her whereabouts, or fate, but without success; when in 1840, Col. Len. Williams, an old and honored Texian, Mr. —— Stoat, a trader, and a Delaware Indian guide, named "Jack Harry," packed mules with goods and engaged in an expedition of private traffic with the Indians.

On the Canadian river they fell in with Pa-ha-u-ka's band of Comanches, with whom they were peaceably conversant. And with this tribe was Cynthia Ann Parker, who from the day of her capture had never seen a white person. She was then about fourteen years of age and had been with the Indians nearly five years.

Col. Williams found the Indian into whose family she had been adopted, and proposed to redeem her, but the Comanche told him all the goods he had would not ransom her, and at the same time "the fierceness of his countenance," says Col. Williams, "warned me of the danger of further mention of the subject." But old Pa-ha-u-ka prevailed upon him to let them see her. She came and sat down by the root of a tree, and while their presence was doubtless a happy event to the poor stricken captive, who in her doleful captivity had endured everything but death, she refused to speak a word. As she sat there, musing, perhaps, of distant relatives and friends, and the bereavements at the beginning and progress of her distress, they employed every persuasive art to evoke some expression. They told her of her playmates and relatives, and asked what message she would send them, but she had doubtless been commanded to silence, and with no hope or prospect of return was afraid to appear sad or dejected, and by a stocial effort in order to prevent future bad treatment, put the best face possible on the matter. But the anxiety of her mind was betrayed by the perceptible quiver of her lips, showing that she was not insensible to the common feelings of humanity.

As the years rolled by Cynthia Ann speedily developed the charms of womanhood, as with the dusky maidens of her companionship she performed the menial offices of drudgery to which savage custom consigns women,—or practiced those little arts of coquetry maternal to the female heart, whether she be a belle of Madison Square, attired in the most elaborate toilet from the *elite* bazars of Paris, or the half naked savage with matted locks and claw-like nails.

Doubtless the heart of more than one warrior was pierced by the Ulyssean darts from her laughing eyes, or charmed by the silvery ripple of her joyous laughter, and laid at her feet the game taken after a long and arduous chase among the Antelope Hills.

Among the number whom her budding charms brought to her shrine was Peta Nocona, a Comanche war chief, in prowess and renown the peer of the famous and redoubtable "Big Foot," who fell in a desperately contested hand-to-hand encounter with the veteran ranger and Indian fighter, Captain S. P. Ross, now living at Waco, and whose wonderful exploits and deeds of daring furnished themes for song and story at the war dance, the council, and the camp-fire.

Cynthia Ann,—stranger now to every word of her mother tongue save her own name—became the bride of Pata Nocona, performing for her imperious lord all the slavish offices which savageism and Indian custom assigns as the duty of a wife. She bore him children, and we are assured *loved* him with a species of fierce passion, and wifely devotion; "for some fifteen years after her capture," says Victor M. Rose, "a party of white hunters, including some friends of her family, visited the Comanche encampment on the upper Canadian, and recognizing Cynthia Ann—probably through the medium of her name alone, sounded her in a secret manner as to the disagreeableness of a return to her people and the haunts of civilization. She shook her head in a sorrowful negative, and pointed to her little, naked barbarians sporting at her feet, and to the great greasy, lazy buck sleeping in the shade near at hand, the locks of a score of scalps dangling at his belt, and whose first utterance upon arousing would be a stern command to his meek, pale-faced wife. Though in truth, exposure to sun and air had browned the complexion of Cynthia Ann almost as intensely as were those of the native daughters of the plains and forest.

She retained but the vaguest remembrance of her people—as dim and flitting as the phantoms of a dream; she was accustomed now to the wild life she led, and found in its repulsive features charms which "upper tendom" would have proven totally deficient in :—"I am happily wedded," she said to these visitors. "I love my husband, who is good and kind, and my little ones, who, too, are his, and I cannot forsake them!"

*   *   *   *   *   *   *   *

What were the incidents in the savage life of these children which in after times became the land marks in the train of memory, and which with civilized creatures serves as incentives to reminiscence?

"Doubtless," says Mr. Rose, "Cynthia Ann arrayed herself in the calico borne from the sacking of Linville, and fled with the discomfited Comanches up the Gaudaloupe and Colorado, at the ruthless march of John H. Moore, Ben McCulloch and their hardy rangers. They must have been present at the battle of Antelope Hills, on the Canadian, when Col. John S. Ford, "Old Rip" and Captain S. P. Ross encountered the whole force of the Comanches, in 1858; perhaps John Parker was an actor in that celebrated battle; and again at the Wichita."

"Their's must have been a hard and unsatisfactory life—the Comanches are veritable Ishmaelites, their hands being raised against all men, and every man's hand against them. Literally, "eternal vigilance was the price of liberty" with them, and of life itself. Every night the dreaded surprise was sought to be guarded against; and every copse was scanned for the anticipated ambuscade while upon the march. Did they flount the blood-drabbled scalps of helpless whites in fiendish glee, and assist at the cruel torture of the unfortunate prisoners that fell into their hands? Alas! forgetful of their race and tongue, they were thorough savages, and acted in all particulars just as their Indian comrades did. Memory was stored but with the hardships and the cruelties of the life about them; and the stolid indifference of mere animal existence furnishes no finely wrought springs for the rebound of reminiscence.''

*   *   *   *   *   *   *   *

The year 1846, one decade from the fall of Parker's Fort, witnessed the end of the Texian Republic, in whose councils Isaac Parker served as a senator, and the blending of the *Lone Star* with the gallaxy of the great constellation of the American Union;—during which time many efforts were made to ascertain definitely the whereabouts of the captives, as an indispensable requisite to their reclamation; sometimes by solitary scouts and spies, sometimes through the medium of negotiation; and sometimes by waging direct war against their captors,—but all to no avail.

*   *   *   *   *   *   *   *

Another decade passes away, and the year 1856 arrives. The hardy pioneers have pushed the frontier of civilization far to the north and west, driving the Indian and the buffalo before them. The scene of Parker's Fort is now in the heart of a dense population; farms, towns, churches, and school houses lie along the path by which the Indians marched from their camp at the ''water-hole'' in that bloody May of 1836.

Isaac Parker is now a Representative in the Legislature of the State of Texas.   It is now twenty years since the battle of San Jacinto; twenty years since John and Cynthia Ann were borne into a captivity worse than death; the last gun of the Mexican war rung out its last report over the conquered capital of Mexico ten long years ago; but John and Cynthia Ann Parker have sent no tokens to their so long anxious friends that they even live: Alas! time even blunts the edge of anxiety, and sets bounds alike to the anguish of man, as well as to his hopes.

The punishment of Prometheas is not of this world!

CHAPTER III.

The Battle of Antelope Hills.

"Brave Colonel Ford the commander and ranger bold,
On the South Canadian did the Comanches behold,
On the 12th of May, at rising of sun,
The armies did meet and the battle begun."

The battle of the South Canadian or "Antelope Hills," fought in 1858, was probably one of the most splendid scenic exhibitions of Indian warfare ever enacted upon Texas soil. This was the immemorial home of the Comanches; here they sought refuge from their marauding expeditions into Texas and Mexico; and here, in their veritable "city of refuge," should the adventurous and daring rangers seek them, it was certain that they would be encountered in full force— Pohebits Quasho—"Iron Jacket," so called from the fact that he wore a coat of scale mail, a curious piece of ancient armor, which doubtless had been stripped from the body of some unfortunate Spanish Knight slain, perhaps, a century before—some chevalier who followed Coronado, De Leon, La Salle—was the war chief. He was a "Big Medicine" man, or Prophet, and claimed to be invulnerable to balls and arrows aimed at his person, as by a necromantic puff of his breath the missives were diverted from their course, or charmed, and made to fall harmless at his feet.

Peta Nocono, the young and daring husband of Cynthia Ann Parker, was second in command.

About the 1st of May, in the year above named, Col. John S. Ford, ("Old Rip,") at the head of 100 Texian Rangers—comprising such leaders as Capts. S. P. Ross, (the father of Gen. L. S. Ross); W. A. Pitts, Preston, Tankersley, and a contingent of 111 Toncahua Indians, the latter commanded by their celebrated chief, Placido—so long the faithful and implicitly trusted friend of the whites—marched on a campaign against the maruding Comanches, determined to follow them up to their stronghold amid the hills of the Canadian river, and if possible surprise them and inflict a severe and lasting chastisement.

After a toilsome march of several days the Toncahua scouts reported that they were in the immediate vicinity of the Comanche encampment. The Comanches, though proverbial for their sleepless vigilance, were unsuspicious of danger; and so unsuspected was the approach of the rangers, that on the day preceding the battle, Col. Ford and Capt. Ross stood in the old road from Fort Smith to Santa Fe, just north of the Rio Negro or "False Wichita," and watched through their glasses the Comanches running buffalo in the valleys still more to the north. That night the Toncahua spies completed the hazardous mission of locating definitely the position of the enemy's encampment. The next morning (May 12) the rangers and "reserve" or friendly Indians, marched before sunrise to the attack.

Placido claimed for his "red warriors" the privilege of wreaking vengeance upon their hereditary enemies. His request was granted,—and the Toncahuas effected a complete surprise. The struggle was short, sharp and sanguinary. The women and children were made prisoners, but not a Comanche brave surrendered. Their savage pride preferred death to the restraints and humiliations of captivity. Not a single warrior escaped to bear the sorrowful tidings of this destructive engagement to their people.

A short time after the sun had lighted the tops of the hills, the rangers came in full view of the hostile camp, pitched in one of the picturesque valleys of the Canadian, and on the opposite side of the stream, in the immediate vicinity of the famous "Antelope Hills."

The panorama thus presented to the view of the rangers was beautiful in the extreme, and their pent-up enthusiasm found vent in a shout of exultation, which was speedily suppressed by Col. Ford. Just at this moment a solitary Comanche was descried riding southward, evidently heading for the village which Placido had so recently destroyed. He was wholly unconcious of the proximity of an enemy. Instant pursuit was now made; he turned, and fled at full speed toward the main camp across the Canadian, closely followed by the rangers. He dashed across the stream, and thus revealed to his pursuers the locality of a safe ford across the miry and almost impassable river. He rushed into the village beyond, sounding the notes of alarm; and soon the Comanche warriors presented a bold front of battle-line between their women and children and the advancing rangers. After a few minutes occupied in forming line of battle, both sides were arrayed in full force and effect. The friendly Indians were placed on the right, and thrown a little forward. Col. Ford's object was to deceive the Comanches as to the character of the attacking force, and as to the quality of arms they possessed.

Pohebits Quasho, arrayed in all the trappings of his "war toggery"—coat of mail, shield, bow and lance, completed by a head-dress decorated with feathers and long red flannel streamers; and besmeared in "war-paint,"—gaily dashed about on his "war-horse" midway of the opposing lines, delivering taunts and challenges to the whites. As the old chief dashed to and fro a number of rifles were discharged at him in point blank range without any effect whatever; which seeming immunity to death encouraged his warriors greatly; and induced even some of the more superstitious among the rangers to enquire within themselves if it were possible that "Old Iron Jacket" really bore a charmed life? Followed by a few of his braves, he now bore down upon the rangers, described a few "charmed circles," gave a few necromantic puffs with his breath and let fly several arrows at Col. Ford, Capt. Ross and chief Placido; receiving their fire without harm. But as he approached the line of the Tonca-huas, a rifle directed by the steady nerve and unerring eye of one of their number, Jim Pockmark, brought the "Big Medicine" to the dust. The shot was a mortal one. The fallen chieftain was instantly sur-rounded by his braves, but the spirit of the conjuring brave had taken its flight to the "happy hunting grounds."

These incidents occupied but a brief space of time, when the order to charge was given; and then ensued one of the grandest assaults ever made against the Comanches. The enthusiastic shouts of the rangers and the triumphant yell of their red allys greeted the welcome order. It was responded to by the defiant "war-hoop" of the Comanches, and in those virgin hills, remote from civilization, the saturnalia of battle was inaugurated. The shouts of enraged combatants, the wail of women, the piteous cries of terrified chil-dren, the howling of frightened dogs, the deadly re-ports of rifle and revolver, constituted a discordant confusion of sounds, blent together in an unearthly mass of infernal noise.

The conflict was sharp and quick—a charge; a mo-mentary exchange of rifle and arrow shots, and the heart-rending wail of discomfiture and dismay, and the beaten Comanches abandoned their lodges and camp to the victors, and began a disorderly retreat. But sufficient method was observed to take advantage of each grove of timber, each hill and ravine, to make a stand against their pursuers; and thus enable the women and children to make their escape.   The noise of battle now diverged from a common center like the spokes of a wheel, and continued to greet the ear for several hours, gradually growing fainter as the pursuit disappeared in the distance.

But another division, under the vigilant Peta Nocona, was soon marching through the hills north of the Canadian, to the rescue.   Though ten miles distant, his quick ear had caught the first sounds of the battle; and soon he was riding, with Cynthia Ann by his side, at the head of (500) five hundred warriors.

About 1 o'clock of the afternoon the last of the rangers returned from the pursuit of Pohebits Quasho's discomfited braves, just in time to anticipate this threatened attack.

As Capt. Ross (who was one of the last to return) rode up, he enquired ''What hour of the morning is it, Colonel?''   ''Morning!'' exclaimed Col. Ford, ''it is one o'clock of the afternoon ;'' so unconscious is one of the flight of time during an engagement, that the work of hours seems comprised within the space of a few moments.

''Hello! what are you in line of battle for?'' asked Ross. "Look at the hills there, and you will see,'' calmly replied Col. Ford, pointing to the hills some half a mile distant, behind which the forces of Peta Nocona were visible; an imposing line of 500 warriors drawn up in battle array.

Col. Ford had with 221 men fought and routed over 400 Comanches, and now he was confronted by a stronger force, fresh from their village still higher up on the Canadian. They had come to drive the "pale faces'' and their hated copper-colored allies from the captured camp, to retake prisoners, to retake over four hundred head of horses and an immense quantity of plunder. They did not fancy the defiant state of preparations awaiting them in the valley, however, and were waiting to avail themselves of some incautious movement on the part of the rangers, when the wily Peta Nocona with his forces would spring like a lion from his lair, and with one combined and desperate effort swoop down and annihilate the enemy. But his antagonist was a soldier of too much sagacity to allow any advantage to a vigilant foe.

The two forces remained thus contemplating each other for over an hour; during which time a series of operations ensued between single combatants illustrative of the Indian mode of warfare, and the marked difference between the nomadic Comanche and his semi-civilized congeners, the Tonchua.   The Tonchuas took advantage of ravines, trees and other natural shelter.   Their arms were rifles and "six-shooters." The Comanches came to the attack with shield and bow and lance, mounted on gaily caparisoned and prancing steeds, and flaunting feathers and all the "georgeous" display incident to savage "finery" and pomp.   They are probably the most expert equestrians in the world.   A Comanche warrior would gaily canter to a point half way between the opposing lines, yell a defiant "war hoop," and shake his shield.   This was a challenge to single combat.

Several of the friendly Indians who accepted such challenges were placed *hors de combat* by their more expert adversaries, and in consequence Col. Ford ordered them to decline the savage banters; much to the dissatisfaction of Placido, who had conducted himself throughout the series of engagements with the bearing of a savage hero.

Says Col. Ford: "In these combats the mind of the spectator was vividly carried back to the days of chivalry; the jousts and tournaments of knights; and to the concomitants of those scenic exhibitions of gallantry.   The feats of horsemanship were splendid, the lances and shields were used with great dexterity, and

the whole performance was a novel show to civilized
man.''

Col. Ford now ordered Placido, with a part of his
warriors, to advance in the direction of the enemy, and if
possible draw them in the valley, so as to afford the
rangers an opportunity to charge them. This had the
desired effect, and the rangers were ready to deliver a
charge, when it was discovered that the friendly Indians had removed the white badges from their heads
because they served as targets for the Comanches, consequently the rangers were unable to distinguish friend
from foe. This necessitated the entire withdrawal of
the Indians. The Comanches witnessed these preparations and now commenced to recoil. The rangers
advanced; the trot, the gallop, the headlong charge,
followed in rapid succession. Lieut. Nelson made a
skillful movement and struck the enemy's left flank.
The Comanche line was broken. A running fight for
three or four miles ensued. The enemy was driven back
wherever he made a stand. The most determined resistance was made in a timbered ravine. Here one of
Placido's warriors was killed, and one of the rangers,
young George W. Pascal wounded. The Comanches
left some dead upon the spot and had several more
wounded. After routing them at this point the rangers
continued to pursue them some distance, intent upon
taking the women and children prisoners; but Peta

Nocona, by the exercise of those commanding qualities which had often before signalized his conduct on the field, succeeded in covering their retreat, and thus allowing them to escape. It was now about 4 P. M., both horses and men were almost entirely exhausted, and Col. Ford ordered a halt and returned to the village.

Brave old Placido and his warriors fought like so many demons. It was difficult to restrain them, so anxious were they to wreak vengeance on the Comanches.

In all of these engagements seventy-five (75) Comanches "bit the dust."

The loss of the rangers was small,—two killed and five or six wounded.

The trophies of Pohebits Quasho, including his lance, bow, shield, head-dress and the celebrated coat of scale mail, was deposited by Col. Ford in the State archives at Austin, where, doubtless, they may yet be seen,—as curious relics of by-gone days.

The lamented old chief, Placido, fell a victim to the revengeful Comanches during the latter part of the great civil war, between the North and South; being assassinated by a party of his enemies on the reservation, near Fort Sill.

The venerable John Henry Brown, some years since, paid a merited tribute to his memory through the columns of the Dallas *Herald.*

Of Placido it has been said that he was the "soul of honor," and "never betrayed a trust." That he was brave to the utmost, we have only to refer to his numerous exploits during his long and gratuitous service on our frontiers. He was implicitly trusted by Burleson and other partisan leaders; and rendered invaluable services in behalf of the early Texian pioneers; in recognition of which he never recieved any reward of a material nature, beyond a few paltry pounds of gun-powder and salt. Imperial Texas should rear a monument commemorative of his memory. He was the more than Tammany of Texas! But I am digressing from the narrative proper.

"Doubtless," says Rose, "Cynthia Ann rode from this ill-starred field with her infant daughter pressed to her bosom, and her sons—two youths of about ten and twelve years of age, at her side,—as fearful of capture at the hands of the hated whites, as years ago—immediately after the massacre of Parker's Fort—she had been anxious for the same."

GENERAL L S ROSS.

CHAPTER IV.

Genl. L. S. Ross.—Battle of the Wichita.

It is not our purpose in this connection, to assume
the role of biographer to so distinguished a personage
as is the chevalier Bayard of Texas—General Lawrence
Sullivan Ross.　That task should be left to an abler
pen ; and besides, it would be impossible to do anything like justice to the romantic, adventurous, and
altogether splendid and brilliant career of the brave and
daring young ranger who rescued Cynthia Ann Parker from captivity, at least in the circumscribed limits of
a brief biographical sketch, such as we shall be compelled to confine ourself to ; yet, some brief mention
of his services and exploits as a ranger captain, by way
of an introduction to the reader beyond the limits of
Texas, where his name and fame are as household
words, is deemed necessary, hence we beg leave here
to give a brief sketch of his life.

"Texas, though her annals be brief," says the
author of "Ross' Texas Brigade," counts upon her
"roll of honor" the names of many heros, living and
dead.　Their splendid services are the inestimable leg-
acies of the past and present, to the future.　Of the
latter, it is the high prerogative of the State to enbalm

their names and memories as perpetual examples to excite the generous emulation of the Texian youth to the latest posterity. Of the former it is our pleasant province to accord them those honors which their services, in so eminent a degree, entitle them to receive. Few lands, since the days of the "Scottish Chiefs," have furnished material upon which to predicate a Douglas, a Wallace, or a Ravenswood; and the adventures of chivalric enterprise, arrant quest of danger, and the personal combat, were relegated, together with the knight's armorial trappings, to the rusty archives of "Tower" and "Pantheon," until the Comanche Bedouins of the Texian plains tendered in bold defiance the savage gauntlet to the pioneer knights of progress and civilization. And though her heraldic roll glows with the names of a Houston, a Rusk, Lamar, McCulloch, Hayes, Chevellie, which illumine the pages of her history with an effulgence of glory, Texas never nurtured on her maternal bosom a son of more filial devotion, of more loyal patriotism, or indomitable will to do and dare, than L. S. Ross."

Lawrence Sullivan Ross was born in the village of Bentonsport, Ohio, in the year 1838. His father, Captain S. P. Ross, emigrated to Texas in 1839, casting his fortunes with the struggling pioneers who were blazing the pathway of civilization into the wilds of a *terra incognita*, as Texas then was.

"Captain S. P. Ross was, for many years, pre-eminent as a leader against the implacable savages, who made frequent incursions into the settlements. The duty of repelling these forays usually devolved upon Captain Ross and his neighbors, and, for many years, his company constituted the only bulwark of safety between the feeble colonist and the scalping knife. The rapacity and treachery of his Comanche and Kiowa foes demanded of Captain Ross sleepless vigilance, acute sagacity, and a will that brooked no obstacle or danger. It was in the performance of this arduous duty that he slew, in single combat, "Big Foot," a Comanche chief of great prowess, and who was for many years the scourge of the early Texas frontier. The services of Captain S. P. Ross are still held in grateful remembrance by the descendants of his compatriots, and his memory will never be suffered to pass away while Texians feel a pride in the sterling worth of the pioneers who laid the foundation of Texas' greatness and glory.— *Vide "Ross' Texas Brigade,"* p. 158.

The following incident, as illustrative of the character and spirit of the man and times, is given: "On one occasion, Captain Ross, who had been visiting a neighbor, was returning home, afoot, accompanied by his little son, 'Sul,' as the General was familiarly called. When within half a mile of his house, he was surrounded by fifteen or twenty mounted Comanche warriors, who commenced an immediate attack. The Captain, athletic and swift of foot, threw his son on his back, and outran their ponies to the house, escaping unhurt amid a perfect shower of arrows.''

Such were among the daily experiences of the child, and with such impressions stamped upon the infantile mind, it was but natural that the enthusiastic spirit of the ardent youth should lead him to such adventures upon the "war-path," similar to those that had signalized his honored father's prowess upon so many occasions.

Hence, we find "Sul" Ross, during vacation from his studies at Florence Weslean University, Alabama, though a beardless boy, scarcely twenty years of age, in command of a contingent of 135 friendly Indians, co-operating with the United States cavalry under the dashing Major Earl Van Dorn, in a compaign against the Comanches.

*   *   *   *   *   *   *   *

Notwithstanding the severe chastisement that had been inflicted on the Comanches at "Antelope Hills," they soon renewed their hostilities, committing many depredations and murders during the summer of 1858.

Early in September Major Van Dorn received orders from Gen. Twiggs, to equip four companies, including Ross' "red warriors," and go out on a scout-

ing expedition against the hostile Indians. This he
did, penetrating the heart of the Indian country where
he proceeded to build a stockade, placing within it all
the pack mules, extra horses and supplies, which was
left in charge of the infantry.

Ross' faithful Indian scouts soon reported the discov-
ery of a large Comanche village near the Wichita
Mountains, about ninety miles away. The four companies, attended by the spies, immediately set out for
the village, and after a fatiguing march of thirty-six
hours, causing the men to be continuously in the saddle
the latter sixteen hours of the ride, arrived in the immediate vicinity of the Indian camp just at daylight on
the morning of October 1st.

A reconnoissance showed that the wily Comanches
were not apprehensive of an attack, and were sleeping
in fancied security. The horses of the tribe, which
consisted of a *caballado* of about 500 head, were grazing near the outskirts of the village. Major Van Dorn
directed Captain Ross, at the head of his Indians, to
"round up" the horses, and drive them from the
camp, which was effected speedily, and thus the Comanches were forced to fight on foot—a proceeding
extremely harrowing to the proud warriors' feelings.

"Just as the sun was peeping above the eastern
horizon," says Victor M. Rose, whose graphic narrative we again quote, "Van Dorn charged the upper

end of the village, while Ross' command, in conjunction with a detachment of United States cavalry, charged the lower. The village was strung out along the banks of a branch for several hundred yards. The morning was very foggy, and after a few moments of firing the smoke and fog became so dense that objects at but a short distance could be distinguished only with great difficulty. The Comanches fought with absolute desperation, and contended for every advantage, as their women and children, and all their possessions, were in peril.

"A few moments after the engagement became general, Ross discovered a number of Comanches running down to the branch, about one hundred and fifty yards from the village, and concluded that they were beating a retreat. Immediately, Ross, Lieutenant Van Camp of the United States Army, Alexander, a 'regular' soldier, and one Caddo Indian, of Ross' command, ran to the point with the intention of intercepting them. Arriving, it was discovered that the fugitives were the women and children. In a moment, another posse of women and children came running immediately past the squad of Ross, who, discovering a little white girl among the number, made his Caddo Indian grab her as she was passing. The little pale-face—apparently about twelve years of age—was badly frightened at finding herself a captive to a strange Indian and stranger white men, and was hard to manage at first.

"Ross now discovered, through the fog and smoke of the battle, that a band of some twenty-five Comanche warriors had cut his small party off from communication with Van Dorn, and were bearing immediately down upon them. They shot Lieutenant Van Camp through the heart, killing him ere he could fire his double-barrelled shot-gun. Alexander, the United States Cavalryman, was likewise shot down before he could fire his gun (a rifle). Ross was armed with a Sharp's rifle, and attempted to fire upon the exultant red devils, but the cap snapped. 'Mohee,' a Comanche warrior, siezed Alexander's rifle and shot Ross down. The indomitable young ranger fell upon the side on which his pistol was borne, and though partially paralyzed by the shot, he turned himself, and was getting his pistol out when 'Mohee' drew his butcher-knife, and started towards his prostrate foe—some fifteen feet away—with the evident design of stabbing and scalping him. He made but a few steps, however, when one of his companions cried out something in the Comanche tongue, which was a signal to the band, and they broke away in confusion. 'Mohee' ran about twenty steps, when a wire-cartridge, containing nine buck-shot, fired from a gun in the hands of Lieutenant James Majors, (afterwards a Confederate General), struck him between the shoulders, and he fell forward on his face, dead. 'Mohee' was an old acquaintance of Ross, as the latter had seen him frequently at his father's post on the frontier, and recognized him as soon as their eyes met. The faithful Caddo held on to the little girl throughout this desperate *melee*, and, strange to relate, neither were harmed. The Caddo, doubtless, owed his escape to the fact that the Comanches were fearful of wounding or killing the little girl. This whole scene transpired in a few moments, and Captain N. G. Evans' company of the Second United States Cavalry, had taken possession of the lower end of the Comanche village, and Major Van Dorn held the upper, and the Comanches were running into the hills and brush; not, however, before an infuriated Comanche shot the gallant Van Dorn with an arrow. Van Dorn fell, and it was supposed that he was mortally wounded. In consequence of their wounds, the two chieftains were compelled to remain on the battle ground five or six days. After the expiration of this time, Ross' Indians made a 'litter,' after their fashion, borne between two gentle mules, and in it placed their heroic and beloved 'boy captain,' and set out for the settlements at Fort Belknap. When this mode of conveyance would become too painful, by reason of the rough, broken nature of the country, these brave Caddos—whose race and history are but synonyms of courage and fidelity—would vie with each other in bearing the burden upon their own shoulders. At Camp Radziminski, occupied by United States forces, an ambulance was obtained, and the remainder of the journey made with comparative comfort. Major Van Dorn was also conveyed to Radziminski. He speedily recovered of his wound, and soon made another brilliant campaign against the Comanches, as we shall see further on. Ross recovered sufficiently in a few weeks so as to be able to return to college at Florence, Alabama, where he completed his studies, and graduated in 1859."

This was the battle of the Wichita Mountains, a hotly contested and most desperate hand to hand fight in which the two gallant and dashing young officers, Ross and Van Dorn, were severely wounded. The loss of the whites was five killed and several wounded.

The loss of the Comanches was, eighty or ninety warriors killed, many wounded, and several captured; besides losing all their horses, camp equipage, supplies, etc.

The return of this victorious little army was hailed with enthusiastic rejoicing and congratulation, and the Wichita fight and Van Dorn and Ross were the themes of song and story for many years along the borders and in the halls and banqueting-rooms of the cities, and the martial music of the "Wichita March" resounded through the plains of Texas wherever the Second

Cavalry encamped or rode off on scouts in after years.

The little girl captive—of whose parentage or history nothing could be ascertained, though strenuous efforts were made—was christened "Lizzie Ross," in honor of Miss *Lizzie* Tinsley, daughter of Dr. D. R. Tinsley, of Waco, to whom Ross at that time was engaged; and afterwards married—May, 1861.

Of Lizzie Ross, it can be said that, in her career, is afforded a thorough verification of Lord Byron's saying: "Truth is stranger than fiction!" She was adopted by her brave and generous captor, properly reared and educated, and became a beautiful and accomplished woman. Here were sufficient romance and vicissitude, in the brief career of a little maiden, to have turned the "roundelay's" of "troubadour and meunesauger." A solitary lily, blooming amidst the wildest grasses of the desert plains. A little Indian girl in all save the Caucasian's conscious stamp of superiority. Torn from home, perhaps, amid the heart-rending scenes of rapine, torture and death. A stranger to race and lineage—stranger even to the tongue in which a mother's lullaby was breathed. Affiliating with these wild Ishmaelites of the prairie—a Comanche in all thingss ave the intuitive premonition *that she was not of them!* Finally, redeemed from a captivity worse than death by a knight entitled to rank, for all

LIZZIE ROSS

time in the history of Texas, *"primus inter pores."*
Vide *"Ross Texas Brigade,"* p. 178.

Lizzie Ross accompanied Gen. Ross' mother on a
visit to the State of California, a few years since, and
while there, became the wife of a wealthy merchant
near Los Angeles, where she now resides.

Such is the romantic story of "Lizzie Ross"—a
story that derives additional interest because of the fact
of its absolute truth in all respects.[1]

(1.—The following letter from Gen. L. S. Ross, touching upon the
battle of the Wichita Mountains and the re-capture of "Lizzie Ross," is
here appropriately inserted:

"WACO, TEXAS, July 12. 1884.

"MR. JAMES T. DESHIELDS.   *Dear Sir*:—My father could give
you reliable data enough to fill a volume. I send you photograph of
Cynthia Ann Parker, with notes relating to her on back of photo. On
the 28th of October, 1858, I had a battle with the Comanches at Wichita
Mts., and there recaptured a little white girl about eight years old,
whose parentage, nor indeed any trace of her kindred, was ever found.
I adopted, reared, and educated her, giving her the name of Lizzie Ross;
the former name being in honor of the young lady—Lizzie Tinsley—to
whom I was then engaged and afterwards married—May, 1861.

"Lizzie Ross grew to womanhood, and married a wealthy merchant
living near Los Angeles, California, where she now resides. See History
of 'Ross' Brigade' by Victor M. Rose, and published by Courier-Jour-
nal, for a full and graphic description of the battle and other notable incidents. I could give you many interesting as well as thrilling adventures of self and father's family with the Indians in the early settlement
of the country.

"He can give you more information than any living Texian, touching the Indian character, having been their agent and warm and trusted
friend, in whom they had confidence.

"My early life was one of constant danger from their forays, and I
was twice in their hands and at their mercy, as well as the other members of my father's family.

"But I am just now too busy with my farm matters to give you such
data as would subserve your purpose.

··Yours truly,   L. S. ROSS."

CHAPTER V.

Battle of Pease River.—Cynthia Ann Parker.

For some time after Ross' victory at the Wichita
Mountains the Comanches were less hostile, seldom
penetrating far down into the settlements. But in
1859–'60 the condition of the frontier was again truly
deplorable. The people were obliged to stand in a continued posture of defense, and were in continual alarm
and hazard of their lives, never daring to stir abroad
unarmed, for small bodies of savages, quick-sighted
and accustomed to perpetual watchfulness, hovered on
the outskirts, and springing from behind bush or rock,
surprised his enemy before he was aware of danger,
and sent tidings of his presence in the fatal blow, and
after execution of the bloody work, by superior knowledge of the country and rapid movements, safely retired to their inaccessable deserts.

In the Autumn of 1860 the indomitable and fearless
Peta Nocona led a raiding party of Comanches
through Parker county, so named in honor of the family of his wife, Cynthia Ann, committing great depredations as they passed through. The venerable Isaac
Parker was at the time a resident of the town of
Weatherford, the county seat; and little did he imagine that the chief of the ruthless savages who spread

desolation and death on every side as far as their arms
could reach, was the husband of his long lost niece;
and that the comingled blood of the murdered Parkers
and the atrocious Comanche now coursed in the veins
of a second generation—bound equally by the ties of
consanguinity to murderer and murdered; that the son
of Peta Nocona and Cynthia Ann Parker would become the chief of the proud Comanches, whose boast
it is that their constitutional settlement of government
is the purest democracy ever originated and administered among men. It certainly conserved the object of
its institution—the protection and happiness of the peo
ple—for a longer period, and much more satisfactorily
than has that of any other Indian tribe. The Comanches claimed a superiority over the other Texian
tribes; and they unquestionably were more intelligent
and courageous. The "Reservation Policy,"—neces-
essary though it be—brings them all to an object level,
—the plane of lazy beggars and thieves. The Comanche is the most qualified by nature for receiving
education and for adapting himself to the requirements
of civilization, of all the southern tribes, not excepting
even the Cherokees, with their churches, school-houses
and farms. The Comanches after waging an unceasing
war for nearly fifty years against the United States,
Texas and Mexico, still number 16,000 souls; a far
better showing than any other tribe can make, though

not one but has enjoyed privileges to which the Comanche was a stranger.   It is a shame to the civilization of the age that a people so susceptible of a high
degree of development should be allowed to grovel in
the depths of heathenism and savagery.   But we are
digressing.

The loud and clamorous cries of the settlers along
the frontier for protection, induced the Government to
organize and send out a regiment under Col. M. T.
Johnson to take the field for public defense.   But these
efforts proved of small service.   The expedition,
though at great expense to the state, failed to find an
Indian until returning, the command was followed by
the wily Comanches, their horses "stampeded" at
night and most of the men compelled to reach the settlements on foot, under great suffering and exposure.

Captain "Sul" Ross, who had just graduated from
Florence Wesleyan University, of Alabama, and returned to Texas, was commissioned a captain of rangers, by Governor Sam Houston, and directed to organize a company of sixty men, with orders to repair to
Fort Belknap, receive from Col. Johnson all government property, as his regiment was disbanded, and
take the field against the redoubtable Peta Nocona, and
afford the frontier such protection as was possible to
this small force.   The necessity of vigorous measures
soon became so pressing that Capt. Ross determined to

attempt to curb the insolence of these implacable
enemies of Texas by following them into their fast-
nesses and carry the war into their own homes. In
his graphic narration of this campaign Gen. L. S. Ross
says: "As I could take but forty of my men from my
post, I requested Capt. N. G. Evans, in command of
the United States troops, at Camp Cooper, to send me
a detachment of the Second Cavalry. We had been
intimately connected on the Van Dorn campaign, during which I was the recipient of much kindness from
Capt. Evans while I was suffering from a severe
wound received from an Indian in the battle of the
'Wichita.' He promptly sent me a sergeant and twenty well mounted men. My force was still further aug-
mented by some seventy volunteer citizens under
command of the brave old frontiersman, Capt. Jack
Cureton, of Bosque county. These self-sacrificing pa-
triots, without the hope of pay or reward, left their de-
defenseless homes and families to avenge the sufferings
of the frontier people. With pack-mules laden down
with necessary supplies the expedition marched for the
Indian country.

"On the 18th of December, 1860, while marching up Pease river, I had some suspicions that Indians
were in the vicinity, by reason of the buffalo that came
running in great numbers from the north towards us,
and while my command moved in the low ground I

visited all neighboring high points to make discoveries.
On one of these sand hills I found four fresh pony
tracks, and being satisfied that Indian videtts had just
gone, I galloped forward about a mile to a higher point,
and riding to the top, to my inexpressable surprise,
found myself within 200 yards of a Comanche village,
located on a small stream winding around the base of
the hill.   It was a most happy circumstance that a
piercing north wind was blowing, bearing with it
clouds of sand, and my presence was unobserved and
the surprise complete.   By signaling my men as I
stood concealed, they reached me without being discovered by the Indians, who were busy packing up pre-
paratory to a move.   By this time the Indians mounted
and moved off north across the level plain.   My command, with the detachment of the Second Cavalry,
had out-marched and become separated from the citizen command, which left me about sixty men.   In
making disposition for attack, the sergeant and his
twenty men were sent at a gallop, behind a chain of
sand hills, to encompass them in and cut off their retreat, while with forty men I charged.   The attack was
so sudden that a considerable number were killed before they could prepare for defense.   They fled precipi-
tately right into the presence of the sergeant and his
men.   Here they met with a warm reception, and
finding themselves completely encompassed, every one

fled his own way, and was hotly pursued and hard pressed.

"The chief of the party, Peta Nocona, a noted warrior of great repute, with a young girl about fifteen years of age mounted on his horse behind him, and Cynthia Ann Parker, with a girl child about two years of age in her arms and mounted on a fleet pony, fled together, while Lieut. Tom. Kelliheir and I pursued them. After running about a mile Killiheir ran up by the side of Cynthia's horse, and I was in the act of shooting when she held up her child and stopped. I kept on after the chief and about a half a mile further, when in about twenty yards of him I fired my pistol, striking the girl (whom I supposed to be a man, as she rode like one, and only her head was visible above the buffalo robe with which she was wrapped) near the heart, killing her instantly, and the same ball would have killed both but for the shield of the chief, which hung down, covering his back. When the girl fell from the horse she pulled him off also, but he caught on his feet, and before steadying himself, my horse, running at full speed, was very nearly upon top of him, when he was struck with an arrow, which caused him to fall to pitching or 'bucking,' and it was with great difficulty that I kept my saddle, and in the meantime, narrowly escaped several arrows coming in quick succession from the chief's bow. Being at such

disadvantage he would have killed me in a few minutes
but for a random shot from my pistol (while I was
clinging with my left hand to the pommel of my saddle) which broke his right arm at the elbow, completely disabling him.   My horse then became quiet, and I
shot the chief twice through the body, whereupon he
deliberately walked to a small tree, the only one in
sight, and leaning against it, began to sing a wild,
wierd song.   At this time my Mexican servant, who
had once been a captive with the Comanches and spoke
their language as fluently as his mother tongue, came
up, in company with two of my men.   I then sum-
moned the chief to surrender, but he promptly treated
every overture with contempt, and signalized this declaration with a savage attempt to thrust me with the
lance which he held in his left hand.   I could only
look upon him with pity and admiration.   For, deplorable as was his situation, with no chance of escape,
his party utterly destroyed, his wife and child captured
in his sight, he was undaunted by the fate that awaited
him, and as he seemed to prefer death to life, I directed the Mexican to end his misery by a charge of buck-
shot from the gun which he carried.   Taking up his
accouterments, which I subsequently sent Gov. Houston, to be deposited in the archives at Austin, we rode
back to Cynthia Ann and Killiheir, and found him bit-
terly cursing himself for having run his pet horse so

hard after an 'old squaw.' She was very dirty, both
in her scanty garments and her person. But as soon
as I looked on her face, I said, 'Why, Tom, this is a
white woman, Indians do not have blue eyes.' On the
way to the village, where my men were assembling
with the spoils, and a large *caballado* of 'Indian
ponies,' I discovered an Indian boy about nine years of
age, secreted in the grass. Expecting to be killed, he
began crying, but I made him mount behind me, and
carried him along. And when in after years I frequently proposed to send him to his people, he steadfastly refused to go, and died in McLennan county last year.

"After camping for the night Cynthia Ann kept crying, and thinking it was caused from fear of death at
our hands, I had the Mexican tell her that we recognized her as one of our own people, and would not
harm her. She said two of her boys were with her
when the fight began, and she was distressed by the
fear that they had been killed. It so happened, however, both escaped, and one of them, 'Quanah' is now
a chief. The other died some years ago on the plains.
I then asked her to give me the history of her life with
the Indians, and the circumstances attending her capture by them, which she promptly did in a very sensi-
ble manner. And as the facts detailed corresponded
with the massacre at Parker's Fort, I was impressed

with the belief that she was Cynthia Ann Parker. Returning to my post, I sent her and child to the ladies at Cooper, where she could recieve the attention her situation demanded, and at the same time dispatched a messenger to Col. Parker, her uncle, near Weatherford, and as I was called to Waco to meet Gov. Houston, I left directions for the Mexican to accompany Col. Parker to Cooper in the capacity of interpreter. When he reached there, her identity was soon discovered to Col. Parker's entire satisfaction and great happiness."

And thus was fought the battle of "Pease river" between a superior force of Comanches under the implacable chief, Peta Nocona on one side, and sixty rangers led by their youthful commander, Capt. L. S. Ross, on the other. Ross, sword in hand, led the furious rush of the rangers; and in the desperate encounter of "war to the knife" which ensued, nearly all the warriors bit the dust.

So signal a victory had never before been gained over the fierce and war-like Comanches; and never since that fatal December day in 1860 have they made any military demonstrations at all commensurate with the fame of their proud campaigns in the past. The great Comanche confederacy was forever broken. The incessant and sanguinary war which had been waged for more than thirty years was now virtually at an end.

The blow was a most decisive one ; as sudden and irresistable as a thunder-bolt, and as remorseless and crushing as the hand of Fate.

It was a short but desperate conflict. Victory trembled in the balance. A determined charge, accompanied by a simultaneous fire from the solid phalanx of yelling rangers and the Comanches beat a hasty retreat, leaving many dead and wounded upon the field. Espying the chief and a chosen few riding at full speed, and in a different direction from the other fugitives, from the ill-starred field, Ross quickly pursued. Divining his purpose, the watchful Peta Nocona rode at full speed, but was soon overtaken, when the two chiefs engaged in a personal encounter, which must result in the death of one or the other. Peta Nocona fell, and his last sigh was taken up in mournful wailings on the wings of defeat. Most of the women and children with a few warriors escaped. Many of these perished on the cold and inhospitable plains, in an effort to reach their friends on the head-waters of the Arkansas river.

The immediate fruits of the victory was some four hundred and fifty horses, and their accumulated winter's supply of food. But the incidental fruits are not to be computed on the basis of dollars and cents. The proud spirit of the Comanche was here broken, and to this signal defeat is to be attributed the measurably pacific conduct of these heretofore implacable foes of the white race during the course of the late civil war in the Union,—a boon of incalculable value to Texas.

In a letter recognizing the great service rendered the state by Ross in dealing the Comanches this crushing blow, Governor Houston said:

"Your success in protecting the frontier gives me great satisfaction. I am satisfied that with the same opportunities, you would rival, if not excel, the greatest exploits of McCulloch and Hays. Continue to repel, pursue, and punish every body of Indians coming into the State, and the people will not withhold their praise." Signed: SAM HOUSTON.

QUANAH PARKER.

CHAPTER VI.

Cynthia Ann Parker.—Quanah Parker.

From May 19th, 1836, to December 18th, 1860, was twenty-four years and seven months. Add to this nine years, her age when captured, and at the later date Cynthia Ann Parker was in her thirty-fourth year. During the last ten years of this quarter of a century, which she spent as a captive among the Comanches, no tidings had been received of her. She had long been given up as dead or irretrievably lost to civilization.

Notwithstanding the long lapse of time which had intervened since the Capture of Cynthia Ann Parker, Ross, as he interrogated his "blue eyed" but bronzed captive, more than suspected that she was the veritable "Cynthia Ann Parker," of which he had heard so much from his boyhood. She was dressed in female attire, of course, according to the custom of the Comanches, which being very similar to that of the males, doubtless, gave rise to the eroneous statement that she was dressed in male costume. So sure was Ross of her identity that, as before stated, he at once dispatched a messenger to her uncle, the venerable Isaac Parker; in the meantime placing Cynthia Ann in charge of Mrs.

Evans, wife of Capt. N. G. Evans, the commandant at Fort Cooper, who at once, with commendable benevolence, administered to her necessities.

Upon the arrival of Col. Parker at Fort Cooper, interrogations were made her through the Mexican interpreter, for she remembered not one word of English, respecting her identity; but she had forgotten absolutely everything, apparently, at all connected with her family or past history.

In dispair of being able to reach a conclusion, Col. Parker was about to leave, when he said, ''The name of my niece was Cynthia Ann.'' The sound of the once familiar name, doubtless the last lingering memento of the old home at the fort, seemed to touch a responsive chord in her nature, when a sign of intelligence lighted up her countenance, as memory by some mystic inspiration resumed its cunning as she looked up, and patting her breast, said, ''Cynthia Ann! Cynthia Ann!'' At the awakening of this single spark of reminiscence, the sole gleam in the mental gloom of many years, her countenance brightened with a pleasant smile in place of the sullen expression which habitually characterizes the looks of an Indian restrained of freedom. There was now no longer any doubt as to her identity with the little girl lost and mourned so long. It was in reality Cynthia Ann Parker,—but, O, so changed!

But as savage-like and dark of complexion as she was, Cynthia Ann was still dear to her overjoyed uncle, and was welcomed home by relatives with all the joyous transports with which the prodigal son was hailed upon his miserable return to the parental roof.

As thorough an Indian in manner and looks as if she had been so born, she sought every opportunity to escape, and had to be closely watched for some time. Her uncle carried herself and child to his home, then took them to Austin, where the secession convention was in session. Mrs. John Henry Brown and Mrs. N. C. Raymond interested themselves in her, dressed her neatly, and on one occasion took her into the gallery of the hall while the convention was in session. They soon realized that she was greatly alarmed by the belief that the assemblage was a council of chiefs, sitting in judgment on her life. Mrs. Brown beckoned to her husband, Hon. John Henry Brown, who was a member of the convention, who appeared and succeeded in reassuring her that she was among friends.

Gradually her mother tongue came back, and with it occasional incidents of her childhood, including a recognition of the venerable Mr. Anglin, and perhaps one or two others.

The civil war coming on soon after, which necessitated the resumption of such primitive arts, she learned to spin, weave and to perform the domestic duties.

She proved quite an adept in such work, and became a very useful member of the household.

The ruling passion of her bosom seemed to be the maternal instinct, and she cherished the hope that when the war was concluded she would at last succeed in reclaiming her two children who were still with the Indians. But it was written otherwise, and Cynthia Ann and her little "barbarian" were called hence ere "the cruel war was over." She died at her brother's in Anderson county, Texas, in 1864, preceded a short time by her sprightly little daughter, "Prairie Flower."

Thus ended the sad story of a woman far famed along the border.

* * * * * * * *

How fared it with the two young orphans we may only imagine. The lot of these helpless ones is too often one of trials, heart-pangs, and want, even among our enlightened people ; and it would require a painful recital to follow the children of Peta Nocona and Cynthia Ann Parker from the terrible fight on Pease river, across trackless prairies, and rugged mountain-ways, in the inhospitable month of December, tired, hungry, and carrying a load upon their hearts far heavier than the physical evils which so harshly beset them. Their father was slain, and their mother a captive. Doubtless they were as intent upon her future recovery, during the many years in which they shared the vicissitudes of their people, until the announcement of her death reached them, as her own family had been for her rescue during her quarter of a century of captivity. One of the little sons of Cynthia Ann died some years after her recapture. The other, now known as Capt. Quanah Parker, born as he says in 1854, is the chief of Comanches, on their reservation in the Indian Territory.

Finally, in 1874, the Comanches were forced upon a "reservation," near Fort Sill, to lead the beggarly life of "hooded harlots and blanketed thieves," and it was at this place that the "war-chief" Quanah, learned that it was possible he might secure a photograph of his mother.[1]

An advertisement to that effect was inserted in the Fort Worth *Gazette*, when General Ross at once forwarded him a copy. To his untutored mind it seemed that a miracle had been wrought in response to his "paper prayer;" and his exclamations, as he gazed intently and long upon the faithful representation of "Preloch," or Cynthia Ann, were highly suggestive of Cowper's lines on his mother's picture; and we take

(1—Mr. A. F. Corning was at Fort Worth in 1862, when Cynthia Ann Parker passed through there. He (Mr. C.) prevailed on her to go with him to a daguerreotype gallery (there were no photographs then) and have her picture taken. Mr. Corning still has this daguerreotype, and says it is an excellent likeness of the woman as she looked then. It is now at the Academy of Art, Waco, and several photographs have been taken from it, one of which was sent to Quanah Parker, and another to the writer, from which the frontispiece to this work was engraved.

the liberty of briefly presenting a portion of the same
in verse:

> My mother! and do my weeping eyes once more—
> Half doubting—scan thy cherished features o'er?
>
> Yes, 'tis the pictured likeness of my dead mother,
> How true to life!   It seems to breathe and move;
>
> Fire, love, and sweetness o'er each feature melt;
> The face expresses all the spirit felt;
>
> Here, while I gaze within those large, dark eyes,
> I almost see the living spirit rise;
>
> While lights and shadows, all harmonious, glow,
> And heavenly radiance settles on that brow.
>
> What is the "medicine" I must not know,
> Which thus can give to death life's bloom and glow.
>
> O, could the white man's magic art but give
> As well the happy power, and bid her live!
>
> My name, me thinks, would be the first to break
> The seal of silence, on those lips, and wake
>
> Once more the smile that charmed her gentle face,
> As she was wont to fold me in her warm embrace.
>
> Yes, it is she, "Preloch," Nocona's pale-faced bride,
> Who rode, a matchless princess, at his side,
>
> 'Neath many a bloody moon afar,
> O'er tortuous paths devoted alone to war.
>
> Long since she's joined him on that blissful shore,—
> Where parting and heart-breakings are no more,—
>
> And since our star with *him* went down in gloom,
> No more to shine above the blighting doom,
>
> 'Neath which my people's hopes, alas, are fled,
> I, too, but long that silent path to tread,—
>
> A child, to be with her and him again,
> Healed every wound an orphan's heart can pain!

Quanah Parker is a Nocone, which means wanderer, but on the capture of his mother, Preloch, and death of his father, Quanah was adopted and cared for by the Cohoites, and when just arrived at manhood, was made chief by his benefactors on account of his bravery. His name before he became a chief was Cepe. He has lived among several tribes of the Comanches. He was at one time with the Cochetaker, or Buffalo Eaters, and was the most influential chief of the Penatakers. Quanah is at present one of the four chiefs of the Cohoites, who each have as many people as he has. The Cohoite Comanches were never on a reservation until 1874, but are to-day further advanced in civilization than any Indians on the "Comanche reservation." Quanah speaks English, is considerably advanced in civilization, and owns a ranche with considerable live stock and a small farm ; wears a citizen's suit, and conforms to the customs of civilization—withal a fine-looklng and dignified son of the plains. In 1884, Quanah, in company with two other prominent Comanche chiefs, visited Mexico. In reporting their passage through that city, the San Antonio *Light* thus speaks of them :

"They bear relationship to each other of chief and two subordinates. Quanah Parker is the chief, and as he speaks very good English, they will visit the City of Mexico before they return. They came from Kiowa, Comanche and Wichita Indian Agency, and Parker bears a paper from Indian Agent Hunt that he, Parker, is a son of Cynthia Ann Parker, and is one of the most prominent chiefs of the half-breed Comanche tribe. He is also a successful stock man and farmer. He wears a citizen's suit of black, neatly fitting, regular "tooth-pick" dude shoes, a watch and gold chain and black felt hat. The only peculiar item in his appearance is his long hair, which he wears in two plaits down his back. His two braves also wear civilization's garb. But wear heavy boots, into which their trousers are thrust in true western fashion. They speak nothing but their native language."

In 1885 Quanah Parker visited the World's Fair at New Orleans.

The following extract from the Fort Worth *Gazette*, is a recent incident in his career:

"HE BLEW OUT THE GAS"

AND ON THAT BREATH THE SOUL OF YELLOW BEAR FLEW TO ITS HAPPY HUNTING GROUNDS.

Another Instance in Which the Noble Red Man Succumbs to the Influence of Civilization!

"A sensation was created on the streets yesterday by the news of a tragedy from asphyxiation at the Pickwick hotel, of which two noted Indians, Quanah Parker and Yellow Bear, were the victims. *   *   *

"The circumstances of the unfortunate affair were very difficult to obtain because of the inability of the

only two men who were possessed of definite information on the subject to reveal it—one on account of
death, and the other from unconsciousness.   The Indians arrived here yesterday from the Territory, on the
Fort Worth & Denver incoming train.   They register-
ed at the Pickwick and were asigned an apartment together in the second story of the building.   *   *
Very little is known of their subsequent movements,
but from the best evidence that can be collected it appears that Yellow Bear retired alone about 10 o'clock,
and that in his utter ignorance of modern appliances, he
blew out the gas.   Parker, it is believed, did not seek
his room until 2 or 3 o'clock in the morning, when, not
detecting from some cause the presence of gas in the
atmosphere, or not locating its origin in the room, he
shut the door and scrambled into bed, unmindful of
the deadly forces which were even then operating so
disastrously.   *   *   *   *

"The failure of the two Indians to appear at breakfast
or dinner caused the hotel clerk to send a man around
to awake them.   He found the door locked and was
unable to get a response from the inmates.   The room
was then forceably entered, and as the door swung back
the rush of the deathly perfume through the aperture
told the story.   A gastly spectacle met the eyes of the
hotel employes.   By the bedside in a crouched position, with his face pressed to the floor, was Yellow

Bear, in the half-nude condition which Indian fashion in night clothes admits. In the opposite corner near the window, which was closed, Parker was stretched at full length upon his back. Yellow Bear was stone dead, while the quick gasps of his companion indicated that he was in but a stone's throw of eternity. The chief was removed to the bed, and through the untiring efforts of Drs. Beall and Moore his life has been saved.

"Finding Quanah sufficiently able to converse, the reporter of the *Gazette* questioned him as to the cause of the unhappy occurrence, and elicited the following facts:

" 'I came,' said the chief, 'into the room about midnight, and found Yellow Bear in bed. I lit the gas myself. I smelt no gas when I came into the room. When I went to bed I turned the gas off. I did not blow it out. After a while I smelt the gas, but went to sleep. I woke up and shook Yellow Bear and told him 'I'm mighty sick and hurting all over.' Yellow Bear says, 'I'm mighty sick, too.' I got up, and fell down and all around the room, and that's all I know about it.'

" 'Why didn't you open the door?' asked the reporter.

" 'I was too crazy to know anything,' replied the chief. * * * * *

"It is indeed, a source of congratulation that the chief will recover, as otherwise his tribe could not be made to understand the occurrence, and results detrimental to those having interests in the Territory would inevitably follow."

The new town of Quanah, in Hardeman county, Texas, was named in honor of chief Quanah Parker.

We will now conclude our little work by appending the following letter, which gives a true pen portrait of the celebrated chief as he appears at his home on the "reservation :"

"ANADARKO, I. T., Feb. 4, 1886.

"* * * *

"* * * *

"We visited Quanah in his teepe. He is a fine specimen of physical manhood, tall, muscular—as straight as an arrow; gray, look-you-straight-through-the-eyes, very dark skin, perfect teeth, and a heavy, raven-black hair—the envy of feminine hearts—he wears hanging in two rolls wrapped around with red cloth. His hair is parted in the middle; the scalp-lock is a portion of hair the size of a dollar, plaited and tangled, signifying: 'If you want fight you can have it.'

"Quanah is how camped with a thousand of his subjects at the foot of some hills near Anadarko. Their white teepes, and the inmates dressed in their bright blankets and feathers, cattle grazing, children playing, lent a wierd charm to the lonely, desolate hills, lately devastated by prairie fire. * * * *

"He has three squaws, his favorite being the daughter of Yellow Bear, who met his death by asphyxiation at Fort Worth in December last. He said he gave seventeen horses for her. His daughter Cynthia, named for her grandmother, Cynthia Parker, is an inmate of the Indian Agent's house. Quanah was attired in a full suit of buck-skin tunic, leggins and moccasins elaborately trimmed in beads—a red breech-cloth, with ornamental ends hanging down. A very handsome and expensive Mexican blanket was thrown around his body; in his ears were little stuffed birds. His hair done with the feathers of bright plumaged birds. He was handsomer by far than any Ingomar the writer has ever seen—but there was no squaw fair enough to personate his Parthenia. His general aspect, manners, bearing, education, natural intelligence, show plainly that white blood trickles through his veins. When traveling he assumes a complete civilian's outfit—dude collar, watch and chain—takes out his ear-rings—he of course cannot cut off his long hair, saying that he could no longer be 'big chief.' He has a handsome carriage; drives a pair of matched grays, always traveling with one of his squaws (to do the chores). Minna-a-ton-ccha is with him now. She knows no English, but while her lord is conversing, gazes, dumb with admiration, at 'my lord'—ready to obey his slightest wish or command."

E
99
.C88
G6

CITY COLLEGE LIBRARY
1825 MAY ST.
BROWNSVILLE, TEXAS 78520

Gowanlock
Two months in the camp
of Big Bear

LEARNING RESOURCE CENTER
1825 May St. Ft. Brown
Brownsville, Texas 78520

BROWNSVILLE PUBLIC
CAMERON COUNTY
PAN AMERICAN UNIVERSITY BROWNSVILLE
TEXAS SOUTHMOST COLLEGE